Twayne's English Authors Series

Sylvia E. Bowman, *Editor*

INDIANA UNIVERSITY

Ford Madox Ford

(TEAS) 55

Ford Madox Ford

By Charles G. Hoffmann

University of Rhode Island

Twayne Publishers, Inc.   ::   New York

Preface

Grandson of Ford Madox Brown the pre-Raphaelite painter, son of Dr. Francis Hueffer the music critic of the London *Times*, and nephew of William Michael Rossetti, Ford Madox Hueffer from his youth was, in his own words, "being trained for a genius" and expected to achieve an important career in the arts. But what career? At eighteen he had published a children's fairy tale (*The Brown Owl*), at nineteen a novel (*The Shifting of the Fire*), at twenty a volume of poems (*The Questions at the Well*), at twenty-three a biography of his grandfather (*Ford Madox Brown*), at twenty-nine a critical essay on the art of Dante Gabriel Rossetti, and at thirty-five he became editor of the literary magazine, the *English Review*. Thus poet, editor, art critic, biographer—Ford was all of these, as well as novelist; but it is as a novelist that his particular genius as a writer flourished and flowered. That is why I have chosen to limit this study to a detailed account and analysis of Ford's novels, of which he wrote thirty; for it is on the basis of such masterpieces of the modern novel as *The Good Soldier* and the tetralogy *Parade's End* that Ford's reputation as a writer largely rests.

If Ford had never written a word, his place in the history of modern letters would be secure, for as editor of the *English Review* (1908-9) and particularly as editor of *transatlantic review* (1924-25), Ford published such writers as Joseph Conrad, Henry James, Arnold Bennett, Norman Douglas, H. G. Wells, John Galsworthy, D. H. Lawrence, E. E. Cummings, Ernest Hemingway, Gertrude Stein, James Joyce, Ezra Pound, William Carlos Williams, John Dos Passos, and Dorothy Richardson, some of them for the first time. Like his character George Moffat in *The Benefactor*, Ford "had the gift for discovering new talent." As he wrote in *It Was the Nightingale*, "For me all manuscripts by unknown writers are wonderful until I open them and every time that I open one I have a thrill of anticipation." But, unlike Moffat, Ford was able to continue with his own writing despite the demands on his time and the financial difficulties of running the magazines.

However, I have not presented Ford's career as an editor because I considered it would be repetitious to treat of biographical details. Instead, I call the reader's attention to Violet Hunt's *I Have This to Say* and to Douglas Goldring's *South Lodge* and *Trained for Genius*, which amply detail Ford's editorship of the *English Review* and *transatlantic review*. Also, Frank MacShane's *The Life and Works of Ford Madox Ford* will provide the reader with a more recent source of information on Ford's career as an editor.

Although Ford published many volumes of poetry throughout his literary career, he never achieved a reputation as a poet. His early poems, those published before the war, are generally traditional and derivative. His war poems render the reality of immediate experience, but they are overshadowed by the more successful rendering of that experience in *Parade's End*. The mud image which recurs throughout the "poems written on active service" is a more fully realized and significant image in *Parade's End*. His late poems show little evidence of development in poetic technique and theme. All this is to say that Ford was essentially a prosateur rather than a poet. Ford himself wrote in his volume of reminiscences, *Thus to Revisit*, "Prose is for me an instrument—like a tool of precision. But the moment I come to want to write about verse I feel—possibly doubts, possibly misgivings; certainly some of the diffidence of the novice." It is as a novelist rather than as a poet that Ford's reputation will endure.

As a literary and art critic Ford was impressionistic in Walter Pater's meaning of the word—that it is the function of the critic to give his impressions about a work of art, not merely as a personal opinion but "to know one's own impression as it really is, to discriminate it, to realize it distinctly" by studying the work of art itself. Ford's critical essay on Hans Holbein the Younger, for example, is an impressionistic study, viewing him as "a great Renderer" who was able to project feeling and mood objectively in his portraits.

But it would be misleading to suggest that Ford's approach is purely impressionistic, for the main "thesis" of his short critical study is that Holbein represented the beginning of the Renaissance—"the age of doubts, of merchants, of individual freedom, of broader ideals, of an opening world and new hopes"—in contrast to Dürer, who represented the old world and old faith of the Middle Ages. Similarly, in his literary study, *The English Novel*, Ford deliberately avoided the literary historian's traditional approach of historical factualism and chronological summary. Instead, he sought to render his impressions of the developments in the English novel from Defoe to Conrad by making broad, suggestive statements that would stimulate the reader to think for himself and compare his own experience as a reader of novels with Ford's.

Both this short study of the English novel and the monumental *March of Literature* show Ford's predilection for the art novel and his concern with technique. They also show, as do most of his autobiographical and biographical reminiscences, a lack of concern for factual accuracy, a tendency which makes Ford notoriously unreliable in statements of fact. A clue to Ford's critical approach is found in the preface to his "biography" of Conrad: if a novel is the biography of a man, then the biography of a man is a novel, and inaccuracies of fact are unimportant, for what matters is "the truth of the impression as a whole."

Of particular importance among Ford's critical works is his impressionistic study of Henry James (1913), in which he pays tribute to James as "the greatest of living writers." Although too diffusive to be more than an appreciation, it deserves an important place in the history of Jamesian criticism as one of the earliest studies of James's mastery of the art of the novel. It is significant that Ford singles out impressionism as the main technique of James's art and that he shows that James's *nouvelles* are above all "the consideration of an 'affair.'" In his early novels Ford was also influenced to some extent by James's style, but I would not go as far as R. W. Lid who, in his critical study, *Ford Madox Ford: The Essence of His Art*, suggests that Ford's apprenticeship was prolonged by too facile an imitation of Jamesian dialogue. It was the early pattern of alternation between novels of social and political satire and historical novels that contributed more to the prolongation of Ford's apprenticeship by tending to diffuse his genius for rendering an affair. However inhibiting James's style may have been at first, the more lasting contributions of James's influence on Ford are the technique of impressionism and the form of the "affair."

My own critical approach to Ford—I hope with an un-Fordian accuracy of fact as well as truth of impression—has been to trace the genesis and development of Ford's art of the novel leading to *The Good Soldier* and *Parade's End*, which are undoubted masterpieces of the modern novel. In my analyses of the novels I have emphasized his techniques, dominant themes, and portrayal of characters. The organization of this study is generally chronological; however, I have changed the chronological sequence where necessary for continuity of discussion—as in the chapter on the novels of collaboration with Conrad—or where illuminating for purposes of comparison, as in the discussion of *The "Half Moon"* and *The Portrait* in Chapter Two.

The titles for Chapters Two and Three are taken from Ford's dedicatory letter to *The Good Soldier*, in which Ford deprecates his early novels as *pastiches*, in comparison to his "great auk's egg," *The Good Soldier*, in which he tried to put all he knew about writing. Only in the sense that all of Ford's earlier novels suffer by comparison with *The Good Soldier* are they *pastiches*. The intent of Chapter Two is to show that the early novels form a pattern of development that constitutes an apprenticeship: an exploration of techniques, themes, and character types that coalesces in the achievement of *The Good Soldier*. The "great auk's egg" was "laid" not because Ford suddenly decided to put all he knew about writing into it, as though he could have done so at any time before if he had really tried, but because he had reached the point of development and maturity to produce a masterpiece.

The title for Chapter Four is taken from a letter Ford wrote in 1931, in which he states that *The Good Soldier* is his best book technically *unless* one reads *Parade's End* as one novel, "in which case the whole design appears." The intent of Chapter Four is to show that *Parade's End* is a successful multiple novel and should be read as one novel in order to understand more fully Ford's artistic achievement. The interrelationship of the four volumes of *Parade's End*—an interrelationship of themes, characters, images, and structural patterns—is "the whole design" by which the tetralogy becomes a single novel, an epical "biography" of Christopher Tietjens.

Conscious of the fact that many of Ford's novels are unfortunately out of print, I have included a minimal but necessary

Preface

amount of plot summary to aid the reader. But with the recent republication of the *Fifth Queen* trilogy in both England and America, there is hope that all of Ford's novels will eventually again be in print. A revival of interest in Ford both by the general reader and by the critic is evident in the republication of some of his works, in the recent publication of a critical biography of Ford by Frank MacShane, the publication of a volume of Ford's letters edited by Richard M. Ludwig, and in the fact that six major critical studies of his novels have been published since 1961. It is hoped that this study will serve as an introduction to Ford's novels as a whole and that it will encourage the reader to read more widely in Ford.

I wish to acknowledge the publishers, Alfred A. Knopf, Inc., for their kind permission to quote from *The Good Soldier* and *Parade's End.* I also wish to acknowledge my grateful appreciation for Sylvia Bowman's constructive and judicious editing of this manuscript. And I wish to acknowledge in some small measure the immeasurable help and encouragement my wife gave me in seeing this book through to print.

University of Rhode Island
Kingston, Rhode Island

Contents

Chronology

1872   Marriage of Dr. Franz Xaver Hüffer (Francis Hueffer), German scholar and music critic of the London *Times*, to Catherine Ernely Madox Brown, daughter of Ford Madox Brown, eminent pre-Raphaelite painter.

1873   Ford Hermann Hueffer born December 17, Merton, Surrey.

1881-   Attended Praetoria House, Folkestone. With death of
1889   father in 1889, attended University College School (London) as day-boy studying music.

1891   Publication of *The Brown Owl*, a children's fairy tale. On visit to relatives in Paris, received into Roman Catholic Church at age eighteen.

1892   Publication of first novel, *The Shifting of the Fire*.

1893   Publication of volume of poems, *The Questions at the Well*, under pseudonym of "Fenil Haig."

1894   Eloped with Elsie Martindale, classmate at Praetoria House; lived in Kent until 1903 (separated, order against Hueffer for Restitution of Conjugal Rights, 1910).

1896   Publication of biography of grandfather, *Ford Madox Brown*.

1898-   Introduced to Joseph Conrad by Edward Garnett, agreed
1909   to collaborate: *The Inheritors* (1901), *Romance* (1903), *The Nature of a Crime* (1909 in the *English Review*; 1924).

1902   Publication of *Rossetti*, art criticism and biography.

1904-   Breakdown of health, travelled on Continent.
1906

1905   *The Benefactor; Hans Holbein.*

1906   *The Fifth Queen*, first of the "Katherine Howard" trilogy.

1907   *Privy Seal, An English Girl,* and *The Pre-Raphaelite Brotherhood.*

1908   *The Fifth Queen Crowned; Mr. Apollo.*

1908- Editor of the *English Review* (twelve issues).
1910

1908- Lived with Violet Hunt at South Lodge during this period
1915   plus short time after World War I (worked on *English Review* and collaborated on *The Desirable Alien* [1913] and *Zeppelin Nights* [1915]).

1909   *The "Half Moon."*

1910   *A Call; The Portrait.*

1911   *The Simple Life Limited; Ladies Whose Bright Eyes.*

1912   *The Panel; The New Humpty-Dumpty.*

1913   *Mr. Fleight; The Young Lovell; Henry James,* critical essay.

1915   *The Good Soldier.*

1915- Commissioned officer in the Welsh Regiment with rank
1919   of 2nd lieutenant. Active service in France; severely gassed.

1919   Changed name from Hueffer to Ford; tried farming in Sussex.

1922   Moved to France; eventually settled in Paris. Rest of life divided between Provence, Paris, and United States (to which he went frequently after 1926).

1923   *The Marsden Case.*

1924   *Joseph Conrad: A Personal Remembrance; Some Do Not. . . .*

1924- Editor, *transatlantic review.*
1925

1925   *No More Parades.*

1926   *A Man Could Stand Up—.*

1928   *The Last Post; A Little Less Than Gods.*

1929   *No Enemy.*

Chronology

1931 *When the Wicked Man; Return to Yesterday.*

1933 *The Rash Act; It Was the Nightingale.*

1934 *Henry for Hugh.*

1936 *Vive Le Roy; Collected Poems.*

1937 Lecturer in comparative literature at Olivet College, Michigan; received honorary doctor of letters degree.

1939 Died at Deauville, France, June 26.

Ford Madox Ford

CHAPTER 1

"We Agreed That . . .":
Ford's Collaboration with Conrad

FORD MADOX FORD first met Joseph Conrad in 1898, and at Conrad's suggestion they began to collaborate in writing fiction, producing, however, in that period from 1898 to 1903, only three works, *The Inheritors* (1901), *Romance* (1903), and *The Nature of a Crime* (1924). Their collaboration has been a much misunderstood literary relationship, leading to the legend that Ford, some eighteen years younger than Conrad, fawned on the greater reputation of the master and contributed little to the partnership. It is true that Ford had published only one novel, *The Shifting of the Fire* (1892), before he met Conrad, who had already published three, including the masterful *The Nigger of the "Narcissus."* It is also true that Ford published no fiction of his own during this period of collaboration whereas two of Conrad's major works, *Lord Jim* and *Heart of Darkness*, were published during this time, and Conrad had already begun writing *Nostromo* while he and Ford were completing *Romance*.[1] However, the collaboration *as a working relationship* was one between equals of different temperaments, not a master-disciple relationship between unequals.

By 1898 Conrad had already committed and dedicated himself to a career as a novelist whereas Ford, "trained for a genius" and only twenty-five at the time, had not yet focused on the novel as a medium for his talents. Indeed, at no time in his career did he devote his energies quite so singlemindedly to the novel as did Conrad. Before he met Conrad, he had published, besides the one novel, three children's fairy tales; a biography of his maternal grandfather, Ford Madox Brown; a volume of poetry, *The Questions at the Well* (1893) under the pseudonym of "Fenil Haig"; and some essays on the pre-Raphaelites. During the period of collaboration he published another volume of poetry, *Poems for Pictures* (1900); a historical and descriptive record of Kent and Sussex port towns, *The Cinque Ports* (1900); and a critical biography of Rossetti (1902). It is evident from this summary of his bibliography that Ford had not yet determined the direction of his genius. It is also quite evident in the decade following that Ford had decided to dedicate himself to the novel, for he published fifteen novels in that eleven-year period before *The Good Soldier*, although with his prodigious energies he also found time to write eleven works of non-fiction, a volume of children's fairy tales, five volumes of poetry, and to edit the *English Review*!

The idea of two important novelists collaborating on a novel is an exciting one to contemplate; ideally, one might hope for a literary masterpiece that would be the synthesis of the talents of two creative imaginations, an ideal that Conrad himself envisaged.[2] Unfortunately, none of the collaborative works comes anywhere near that ideal "welded" collaboration Conrad speaks of, nor does there emerge the "third artist" who synthesizes the talents of the two, that both hoped for. All of the collaborative works are lesser novels than any of the three Conrad had already written, to say nothing of the three novels he worked on during that period: *Lord Jim, Heart of Darkness,* and *Nostromo.* However, the collaborations do represent a significant advance in technique for Ford over his first novel. Therefore, the exchange of ideas about the craft and the theory of the novel that took place between Conrad and Ford was of singular importance to the development of Ford as a novelist.

In 1897 Conrad wrote the preface to *The Nigger of the "Narcissus"* which is his credo as a novelist: Fiction, as an art form, "appeals to temperament," and this appeal "must be an impression conveyed through the senses." "My task," Conrad continues in the preface, "is, by the power of the written word, to make you hear, to make you feel—it is, before all, to make you *see*." The condition of art, then, is that every line of a work of fiction should carry its "justification," a term which Ford expanded to include the justification for characters' actions, however minor the character and however minor the action. Thus, Conrad, the year before he met Ford, had stated his theory of the novel; however, like their working relationship as collaborators, it was not a matter of Ford's becoming a disciple and adopting the master's theories as his own. Both Ford and Conrad were influenced by Flaubert's concept of *le mot juste*—the right word which would render the exact impression desired by the writer. Undoubtedly, Ford, as the younger man whose theories of fiction were as yet unformulated, had much to learn from Conrad, just as Ford did from James; but what should be understood is that Ford had a predisposition for Conrad's theories so that the exchange of ideas that took place between them was not one-sided.

Though Ford reacted against the Romantic theories and against the eccentricities of some of the personalities involved in the pre-Raphaelite and esthetic movements, he nonetheless retained a conviction that the artist is a special being and that art is for its own sake. Ford defended the right of the artist to represent life according to his own special vision and rejected Ruskin's belief in the necessity of a moral purpose. Even before Conrad's preface, Ford had been influenced by James's essay, "The Art of Fiction" (1888). In this essay James defined the novel as "a personal, a direct impression of life: that, to begin with, constitutes its value, which is greater or lesser according to the intensity of the impression." Restating this doctrine of impressionism, Ford and Conrad "agreed that the general effect of a novel must be the general effect that life makes on mankind. [. . .] we saw that Life did not narrate, but made impressions on our brains. We in turn, if we wished to produce on you an effect of life, must not narrate but render . . . impressions."[3]

The techniques of impressionism—time shift, fidelity to the point of view of the narrating consciousness, careful selection of details to render the exact impression of perceived experiences, use of pictorial images and symbols, "justification," and *progression d'effet*—were all discussed and developed by Ford and Conrad during those years of close friendship from 1898 to 1909. Conrad had already in his first novel, *Almayer's Folly* (1895), used some of these techniques whereas Ford's first novel exhibits none of the impressionistic techniques found in *The Inheritors,* the first novel of collaboration. Therefore, a comparison of *The Shifting of the Fire* and *The Inheritors* shows a sudden breakthrough in technique; and, since *The Inheritors* was largely Ford's work with Conrad contributing the last twenty pages,[4] the breakthrough is significant in Ford's development as a novelist.

[21]

However, Ford did not change overnight from a youthful apprentice to a mature master of the craft; there are weaknesses in both these early novels which suggest that Ford was groping for mastery of the craft. Indeed, as Wiley has shown, the early novels reveal a gradual development of technique and ideas culminating in the mature artistry of *The Good Soldier*.[5]

The Shifting of the Fire, published when Ford was nineteen, is a Victorian period piece involving an improbable central situation: Edith Ryland, forbidden by her parents to marry her bankrupt fiancé, Clement Hollebone, decides to marry the aged, rich Kasker-Ryves as an idealistic gesture of sacrificial love in the expectation that she will be able to recoup Hollebone's lost fortune when Ryves dies. Her motivation is entirely pure, appearances to the contrary; she believes Ryves will remember her in his will for being a consolation to him in his old age, and she believes she is doing the right thing for love. Perhaps this central situation would have been more plausible if Edith had been less innocent, less idealistic, had been more like Madame Merle in James's *The Portrait of a Lady*; but quite obviously Ford intended to contrast Edith's chivalric code of honor, untainted by any crass materialism, with the mercantile society around her, represented particularly by her father's equation of financial solvency with virtue and social acceptability. Hollebone's willingness to sacrifice his own personal fortune to pay his creditors is the idealistic parallel to Edith's sacrifice; significantly, Mr. Ryland considers Hollebone's gesture an unpardonable piece of "quixotic honesty."

The central symbol gives the novel its title. The symbol occurs literally in the first scene when the smoldering fire shifts and the resulting blaze of light reveals Edith's presence to Hollebone; it illuminates the romantic love between them. It finds its echo in the "smouldering fire" of Edith's eyes when she is forced by her father to write to Hollebone breaking off their engagement (which she refuses to do). It reaches its climax when Edith, confronted by Hollebone's accusation of betrayal of their love, in mental anguish compounded of her husband's mental torture and her own sense of guilt, declares, "I should have gone to hell, but it would only have been a shifting of the fire within my soul to without."[6]

Unfortunately, Ford over-used the literal occurrence of the

symbol: while it is a logical extension of the symbol to suggest that Hollebone had shifted the fire of his passion from Edith to Kate, it is a contrived coincidence to have the fire literally shift at the very moment Hollebone is about to declare his love to Kate, thus reminding him of that first shifting of the fire and revealing to him that he really loves Edith still and not Kate. The fire again literally shifts at the very moment of Ryves's death, and finally near the end, when Hollebone and Edith are together again, the fire shifts, and Hollebone is reminded that, as he believes, Edith poisoned Ryves.

The vial of poison which Hollebone gives to Edith on her birthday, an incredible macabre joke, is a cumbersome attempt by Ford to provide melodramatic suspense in the novel—will she use it to commit suicide?—did she murder her husband?—did he commit suicide? Yet in spite of the awkwardness of the plot machinery involved in keeping the reader in suspense, the vial of poison underscores Ford's groping attempt to develop what was to become one of his major themes: the discrepancy between appearances and reality, a theme which reaches its perfection of treatment in *The Good Soldier* and in *Parade's End.*

The appearance of Edith's marriage to Ryves as a calculated deception to gain wealth and social position, which even Hollebone comes to believe, hides the reality of her romantic idealism; yet she comes to realize that her sacrifice has done harm to Ryves. Ryves appears to be "a fine old English gentleman," his social image unblemished by any breath of scandal; but the reality is that his youth was spent as a libertine, his only son and heir is the illegitimate son of a prostitute, and his monomaniacal scheme of revenge against Edith is the hidden reality of a "diseased" heart motivated by sexual jealousy. Personal integrity, altruism, and romantic idealism all appear to be basely motivated; but in reality they are the truth of Edith's code of honor. Class, wealth, and social respectability appear to be the truth of Ryves's character; but in reality they are the deceptive appearances by which he is judged.

The Shifting of the Fire, though it contains elements of satire in its treatment of business "ethics" and in its portrayal of an upper class corrupted by materialism, is essentially a romantic, not a satiric, novel. The novel ends on a romantic note: the evil of the past is dead, and the good survives in the recognition by

Edith and Hollebone of how much each loved the other—she, by her sacrificial marriage to Ryves; he, by his willingness to marry Edith even though he believed that she had murdered Ryves.

The Inheritors (1901), on the other hand, is essentially a satire utilizing a romantic plot. The subtitle, An Extravagant Story, underscores the fable element of the plot: the notion that a new race, the Fourth Dimensionists, are to inherit the earth must be accepted on the basis of science fiction.

Ford's use of a pseudo-scientific plot as a basis for a political satire must be seen against the background of science-fiction novels published in the late nineteenth century stemming from Jules Verne's series of successful novels of scientific fantasy beginning with Five Weeks in a Balloon (1862). The Inheritors must also be understood in relation to H. G. Wells's series of satiric science fiction, particularly the first, published in 1895, The Time Machine, in which a time machine, based on the theory that time is the fourth dimension, enables investigators to see the future when Darwinian natural selection has evolved such an overly refined type of descendant from the present leisure class that these "Eloi" are easy prey to the cannibalistic, animal-like type descended from the working class. As a result, a million years later the human species is wiped out, and the highest form of life is found to be giant crustaceans.

Wells's evolution-in-reverse theme in The Time Machine, together with its theory of the fourth dimension, may well have provided Ford, who originally sketched the outline of the plot and who wrote most of The Inheritors, with the idea for this political satire written in collaboration with Conrad. However, the basic theme of The Inheritors, that man's ideals—ideas of pity, love, ethics, traditions, even of good form—have become corrupted in a world of practical politics and social hypocrisy is central to Ford's vision of the world as revealed in his novels. The notion that those very ideals make an individual vulnerable to corruption or a prey to others who have been corrupted is at the core of Ford's works, and this concept reaches its culmination in the portraits of Sylvia and Christopher Tietjens in Parade's End.

In The Inheritors, Granger, a writer, has corrupted his ideals by agreeing to do a series of popular portraits of famous people for money. His love for the woman from the Fourth Dimension

[24]

blinds him to the danger she represents to civilization, but more importantly she preys on this weakness in him and uses him as the means by which she is accepted into society as his "sister." That love is an irrational passion which can destroy the moral fiber of a man who has already compromised his ideals is a Conradian theme already found in Conrad's first two novels, *Almayer's Folly* (1895) and *An Outcast of the Islands* (1896).

The love motif and the political satire are interrelated at the end of *The Inheritors*: Granger sacrifices his conscience and betrays his friends by refusing to suppress Callan's exposé of the Greenland scandal in the belief that the woman will now accept him as part of the future because of his love for her. The irony is that he acts exactly as she expected him to out of selfish love for her; she counted precisely on his willingness to betray his friends. He does not belong to the future because his conscience makes him remorseful for what he has done and because his love, never returned by her, is a weakness, an element of self-pity.

The Greenland scandal involved a supposed philanthropic scheme to create a model state in Greenland by bringing the benefits of modern civilization and progress to the Eskimos— railroads, sewing machines, European clothes, abolition of cannibalism and slavery. Though a private venture by the Duc de Mersch, the government is heavily committed to it ideologically and financially by Granger's friend Churchill. The reality, as exposed by Callan, is that the Duc exploited the natives for private profit; the natives were flogged and butchered, and famine, vice, disease, and crime were rampant. As a result of the exposé, the government collapsed, Churchill and Fox were ruined, the small shareholders financially ruined, and the Duc de Mersch and Granger himself were in disgrace. Such a political theme, one can be sure, was close to Conrad's view of English colonialism. By 1899 Conrad had completed writing, though had not yet published, *Heart of Darkness*, which utilizes a similar theme and exposes the horrors of colonial exploitation. But *Heart of Darkness* is a masterful artistic achievement, and *The Inheritors* is a failure.

Paradoxically, the style is the main reason for the failure of *The Inheritors* as a novel of political satire. Paradoxically, because the style of this second novel is remarkably mature in contrast to *The Shifting of the Fire*, a difference which cannot be explained solely on the basis of Conrad's collaboration since most of the novel was written by Ford except for the last twenty pages. In *The Shifting of the Fire* the dialogue is stilted and unrealistic, even at times banal, as when Edith says to herself upon learning that Hollebone's business is in difficulty: "Oh dear! Oh dear! poor Clem, I hope he won't be ruined. It will be such hard lines for him" (20). Ford's attempt to present the thoughts of his characters is at best awkward, his narrative style is immature, and his portrayal of character is derivative and mainly unsubtle. This lack of maturity in style has led one critic to suggest that *The Shifting of the Fire* is a satire on the Victorian novel,[7] but one can best understand the lapses by remembering that Ford was only nineteen when the novel was published. Nine years— the writing of non-fiction and poetry and the first draft of the novel that was to become *Romance*—and the meeting with Conrad separate the two novels.

The Inheritors represents Ford's first application of the theory of impressionism to the novel. It is the impressionistic condensation, as Wiley has pointed out, which defeats the political satire (141); for, unlike Marlow in Conrad's *Heart of Darkness*, Granger in *The Inheritors* is remote from the heart of darkness and can only report his impressions of the horror second and even third hand. Even the general outlines of de Mersch's scheme are reported somewhat vaguely by Granger to the reader, and what is missing—but should not be missing—in such a political satire is the sense of the reality of the horror being revealed. Ironically, the "extravagant" element, the use of the Fourth Dimension idea, can be accepted by the reader on the basis of a willing suspension of disbelief; but the fictional representation of a political scandal must be presented realistically to be plausible. Yet *The Inheritors* is important in the development of Ford's vision of the world as presented in his novels, for it begins, as Wiley points out, "Ford's long study of the decline of a ruling class standard in the face of modern corruption" (142).

Romance was the most thorough collaboration between Ford and Conrad and the most agonized over of the three works. Conrad assigned the authorship of each part in a letter to Ford: "First Part, yours; Second Part, mainly yours, with a little by me on points of seamanship and suchlike small matters; Third

Part, about 60 per cent. mine with important touches by you; Fourth Part, mine with here and there an important sentence by you; Fifth Part practically all yours . . . with perhaps half a dozen lines by me."[8] Though Ford concurred in this assignment of authorship as far as the general plan of the novel was concerned, he pointed out that, "when it comes however to the writing the truth is that Parts One, Two, Three and Five are a singular mosaic of passages written alternately by one or other of the collaborators. The matchless Fourth Part is both in conception and writing entirely the work of Mr. Conrad" (*Nature of a Crime*, 51). It seems, then, that if any one of the collaborative works would achieve that ideal synthesis of two creative imaginations, it would be *Romance*. Unfortunately, it is a disappointing novel, despite being competent enough in its use of suspenseful narration, its rendering of the historical and political situation in Jamaica, its ironic theme, and its impressionistic techniques. It is far less in achievement than *Nostromo* which Conrad had begun in 1903, and it also does little to suggest Ford's development as a historical novelist as represented by the Katharine Howard trilogy (1906-8).

A clue to the failure to achieve an ideal welding of their talents is suggested by Ford himself in his note on *Romance*: "Every collaboration is a contest of temperaments if it be at all thoroughly carried out [. . .]" (*Nature of a Crime*, 51). As Wiley suggests, Conrad's liking for incisiveness clashed with Ford's propensity for "the muted effect" (139). There is an unevenness of style and a straining after an effect which is to be attributed not to one author or the other, but to a "contest of wills" in which "it was the continual attempt on the part of the one collaborator to key up and of the other to key down" (*Nature of a Crime*, 52).

The theme of *Romance* is found in the ironic implications of the title: Romance, to narrator John Kemp, is Adventure, Life; but he demands of fate that he "be gently wafted into the position of a hero of romance."[9] Reality, however, is not so gentle as he stumbles unheroically and accidentally into adventure at the very beginning, and there is real danger involved in his later adventures. The young Kemp has all the romantic illusions of Lord Jim: "Journeying in search of romance—and that, after all, is our business in this world—is much like trying to catch the horizon" (49). The irony lies in the discrepancy between the romantic concept of swashbuckling adventure and the reality of evil actions for material gains and political power and in the discrepancy between Kemp's romantic interpretation of events and the reality of the situations he finds himself in. At the beginning, Kemp mistakenly believes Carlos is a glamorous, romantic pirate; and thus, when he falls into the hands of the real pirates led by O'Brien, he learns they are vultures whose "habits were obscene and nocturnal." He discovers romantic love in Seraphina (the title of Ford's original draft of the novel which he had written before he met Conrad), but he must first destroy the "evil prince," O'Brien, before he can possess her.

Like Lord Jim, Kemp displays a fateful immobility in a crisis that calls for action: his failure to kill Manuel because of an English sense of pity (a Fordian touch) has nearly disastrous consequences, just as Lord Jim's letting Brown go brings disaster. Manuel is finally destroyed by his own fear and superstition, but not until both Kemp and Seraphina have nearly died of thirst and Castro has had to sacrifice his own life to save the other two.

The emphasis in *Romance*, however, unlike *Lord Jim*, is not on the moral and psychological analysis of the protagonist's failure to embody that romantic vision of himself, but on Romance itself: "that subtle thing that is mirage" and yet is life itself. O'Brien is killed by the crazed Salazar, not by the "hero"; and, indeed, Kemp's ill-conceived attempt to find Captain Williams leads quickly to his capture by O'Brien. Though Kemp does not betray Seraphina's whereabouts, he has betrayed her portentous warning never to be separated from her. At the beginning, Kemp believes he must leave England to find Romance; at the end of the Fourth Part, he has come to believe England a romantic place, far away, "an abode of peace, a sanctuary of love." But he is brought home in disgrace and saved only at the last minute from being hanged as a common criminal, a pirate. The novel ends happily, Kemp and Seraphina are reunited, but both have suffered before they can enjoy their romantic happiness: "suffering is the lot of us men" because suffering is "the mark of manhood" bearing "within its pain a hope of felicity like a jewel set in iron" (427).

All three of the collaborative works are narrated in the first person by the protagonist, the same narrative method Ford used in *The Good Soldier*. Like many of Conrad's novels, *Romance* is a novel of action and suspenseful adventure in which reflective passages present a perspective on events; the story is narrated some years later with John Kemp looking back on his romantic youth. Irony is thus achieved by present knowledge of past illusions, a device Ford used extensively in *The Good Soldier* and Conrad in *Heart of Darkness*; but there is also in *Romance* a nostalgic remembrance of "the mystery and promise" of youth. The techniques of impressionism are used, and the scene near the beginning of Part Four in which Kemp, Seraphina, and Castro, enshrouded by fog as they attempt to reach Captain Williams' ship pursued by the pirates, is not only masterfully controlled impressionism, but is also suggestive of Ford's use of the fog in *Some Do Not . . .* , particularly when Manuel sings to guide the pirate boats and Kemp fancies he sees Manuel's "shape in the white vapor, like a shadow thrown from afar by a tallow dip upon a snowy sheet [. . .]" (208).

And during the trial scene all the frustration and helpless sense of injustice engendered by the ironic mistake of identity, Kemp being mistaken for the pirate Nicola, is rendered visually by Kemp's unconsciously jamming his hand on the spike of the prisoner's dock, just as in *The Good Soldier* we are made to "see" the illicit relationship between Florence Dowell and Edward Ashburnham by the touch of her hand on his wrist. Kemp's sense of honor and fair play, which prevent him from killing Manuel and O'Brien and thus involves him in dangerous situations, is suggestive of Tietjens' decency which is used against him.

However, it would be misleading to suggest that *Romance*, or any of the collaborative works, leads directly to the mature achievement of *The Good Soldier* and *Parade's End*. Though there are some reflective passages involving Kemp's looking back on the events of his youth, the narrative is generally a straightforward chronology of events so that the time-shift technique is not used to reinforce the irony. The progress of the narrative is largely determined by the complications of the action itself rather than arising mainly out of the inner necessity of character psychology and morality. Though Kemp's failure to kill Manuel when he has the opportunity does derive from his sense of decency, such a suspenseful complication is common in pure adventure stories; and Kemp's decision to find Captain Williams, which results in his capture and all the complications of the last part of the novel, including the trial, is motivated only by a momentary romantic enthusiasm and by impatience with waiting for the captain's return. The trial itself is an ironic accident of mistaken identity rather than a tragic inevitability, and the scene ends with a conventional last minute reprieve.

Though *Romance* is based on an actual historical situation in early nineteenth-century Jamaica and though Kemp's trial is based on the actual piracy trial of Aaron Smith, the historical and political material, while contributing to the theme of evil and to the verisimilitude of the action, remains essentially a background for romantic adventures and romantic love. Ford was soon to achieve on his own a more authentic and integrated rendering of history through character portrayal in the Katharine Howard trilogy. Nonetheless, *Romance* is a serious novel, not a mere story of adventure; it is an attempt to use the very materials of adventure to explore "the romantic side of our life," for life itself is a romance, a subjective reality, an adventure illuminated by conscience. Ironically, *Romance* is most successful in its scenes of adventurous action, and thus its serious intent is overshadowed by Kemp's romantic adventures.

The Nature of a Crime, unlike *The Inheritors* and *Romance*, was never completed as a novel; it was first published as a short story in the April and May, 1909, issues of the *English Review* and later reprinted in *transatlantic review* in January and February of 1924, before being published with additions in book form later the same year, shortly after Conrad's death. It is a rounded fragment, to use Conrad's words, of a novel intended to treat of, in Ford's words, "the eternal subject of the undetected criminal." As such, it remains an interesting postscript rather than a major achievement of the collaboration between Ford and Conrad. It is in the form of an "analytical confession" by the narrator to his married mistress in Rome that he has for years been embezzling money from the trust fund of which he is sole trustee; the embezzlement will be discovered because Edward Burden, the beneficiary of the trust fund, has ordered an audit of the books, not because he has any suspicions but because he is the kind of person who wants everything legally in order before he takes over. The narrator intends to commit suicide before his

crime is discovered by the auditors, but in the meeting between Burden and the narrator, Burden announces he has called off the audit because it is an insult to the "trust" that Burden's father held for the narrator. We are left with the irony that though the narrator's crime remains undetected by Burden, he has mailed the confession to his mistress, and it is now up to her to expose him or say nothing. It is a "lady or the tiger" ending, a solution that was solely Ford's own; but perhaps it was the only one to round out this fragment without leaving it completely unresolved.

The serious theme of *The Nature of a Crime* is stated but not developed in the only truly dramatic scene of the work: the meeting with Burden. About to be married, Burden confesses that he has had an affair with another woman; his "crime," and it is presented as a worse crime than the narrator's, is that he confesses so that he could "project the sinful effect of that irregular connection [. . .] into his regulated, reformed [. . .] state —for the sake of retrospective enjoyment" and to ease his conscience (20).

The narrator, who from a legal point of view is the criminal while Burden is his victim, accuses Burden of being "the most debauched person I have ever met," not because of the affair itself, but because his motivation is to shift the burden of his immorality to the narrator and thus free himself of any blame: "He expected to be able to say: 'I have sinned,' and to be able to hear the Deity say: 'That's all right, your very frank confession does you infinite credit.' His deity was, in fact, to find him some way out of his moral hole. I was to find him some genial excuse; to make him feel good in his excellent digestion once more" (20). There is a suggestion, a hint, of Edward Ashburnham in the character of Edward Burden; but, unfortunately, his character is not sufficiently developed in this fragment since much of the narrative is concerned with the details of the narrator's crime and with the "justification" for the confession. And there is a faint suggestion of Dowell in the narrator's retrospective analysis, but the portrayal lacks depth.

A postscript to *The Nature of a Crime* is provided by the fact that Ford later published a poem, "Views," a version of the opening passage of the prose work. The poem more explicitly reveals that the purpose of the opening passage is to focus the reader's attention on the fact that the narrator, though he has been this woman's lover for seven years, does not really know her; and, therefore, does not really know what she will do about his confession:

> . . . For, if man knew woman
> I should have plumbed your heart; if woman, man
> Your me should be true I . . .

The Nature of a Crime adds little to Ford's development as a novelist beyond a further exploration of first-person narration with its self-analysis and with its impressionistic approach to experience which comes through momentarily in this work when the narrator is given a new lease on life and when he experiences the common sights of the everyday world with new intensity as though he were "reborn." However, long before Conrad and Ford published this work as a short story in the *English Review*, Ford had struck out on his own as a novelist, publishing seven novels in that short period between 1905 and 1909 besides numerous non-fiction works, including critical studies of Holbein and the Pre-Raphaelite Brotherhood, a volume of poetry, and a three-volume interpretative study of England and the English mind.

CHAPTER 2

"In the Nature of Pastiches":
The Early Novels

I The Benefactor

THE BENEFACTOR (1905), published some thirteen years after *The Shifting of the Fire*, is actually Ford's second novel. It marks the true beginning of his career as a novelist since *The Shifting of the Fire* must ultimately be dismissed as juvenilia, and since no assigning to Ford of specific chapters and passages in the collaborative works with Conrad dispels the shadow of their clashing artistic temperaments which resulted in something less than either was capable of. *The Benefactor* is a beginning not because it represents a major breakthrough in technique or in characterization, but because it represents Ford's first groping toward the form of the novel of his masterpiece, *The Good Soldier*: the rendering of an Affair.

The sub-title of *The Benefactor, A Tale of a Small Circle*, suggests the main element of this form—a few characters who form a tight, small circle so that there is an interaction among the group to any action by one of the characters. Thus the novel becomes "one embroilment, one set of embarrassments, one human coil, one psychological progression."[1] George Moffat, the benefactor and protagonist, is the center of the circle; for it is his "gift for discovering new talent" which sets in motion the embroilment and the progression of the affair.

The central situation of *The Benefactor* involves the discrepancy between the good intentions of a benevolent man of honor and the reality of his actions which cause "an immense amount of misery." This quality of George Moffat's—of causing misery with the best of intentions—makes him a prototype of Christopher Tietjens in *Parade's End*; for, like Tietjens, he muddles through: he is an idealist whose good works and intentions are resented or cause unhappiness in others and are turned against him in the end. Prisoner of a Victorian ethic based on benevolence and self-sacrifice, Moffat is prey to the selfish demands of others on his time and money; and, though he is occasionally tempted to think of himself, he cannot resist the impulse to help others, for with him it is a matter of honor. A poet in his own right, he has been unable to develop his own talents because he is too busy helping other writers get started in their careers: "The pity was that as soon as the men he had helped stood on their own feet they invariably dropped George and generally insulted him."[2] Hailes, George's latest protégé, drops him, having bled him sufficiently and having found another "benefactor" in George's sister-in-law, whose intentions are somewhat less than esthetic.

While George can justify to himself his benefactions as sacrifices for art's sake—it is Hailes's novel, not Hailes himself, that matters to him—the inevitable human embroilment that his benevolence involves, ruins him and causes misery in others. His wife left him years before because of the coterie of young men he gathered around him. Indirectly, he causes the estrangement of his brother Gregory and his wife, because of Hailes. Thwaite, another protégé, bitterly turns against him; and in the end the whole village turns against him, now a bankrupt man, having resented his meddling in their private lives by telling them with the best intentions of helping them what they should do.

The very qualities of his goodness—his generosity, his honor, his self-sacrificing motivations—are the cause of a series of catastrophes. His bankruptcy is the result of his generosity; and, though his financial ruin is ironically reversed by the unexpected financial success of his first novel, which he considers to be unworthy of his talents, he has had to sell the family estate to pay his debts so that the way of life he has known is finished. Thwaite's bitterness is caused by his dismissal from the editorship of the literary magazine, the *Salon*, which Moffat has promised him would never happen; and, in an excess of worry over money, Thwaite has developed brain fever.

But the madness of the Reverend Brede is the final catastrophe. Moffat, giving up precious time from the writing of his novel, devotes himself to trying to cure the psychotic Reverend Brede of a guilt complex based on the belief that he had caused

his wife's death. Convinced that Brede needs to take his mind off his guilt feelings, Moffat encourages him to go back into active ministry; as a result of this over-exertion, the Reverend Brede goes mad in the middle of a sermon. In love with Brede's daughter, Clara, Moffat cannot now bring himself to marry her. In a spirit of self-sacrifice, he renounces personal happiness: "I couldn't make love to his daughter after ruining him" (347). Clara, who had devoted herself first to taking care of her dying mother and then her half-mad father, rebels against the spirit of self-sacrifice: " 'Self-sacrifice,' she said, slowly, 'Doesn't that ever end?' " (349).

But it does not ever end, at least not for the George Moffats of the world, who are driven by an inner necessity to do the honorable thing. Some do not sacrifice honor for personal happiness; and, though those around him whom he has helped have grabbed what they could for themselves, George Moffat is one of those who do not. Ford calls this novel a "Jamesian pastiche," but Moffat is no Jamesian hero morally triumphant in the sacrifice of personal happiness: he is haunted by the image of the old man he has ruined by his meddling as well as by the fear that he would destroy Clara's reputation because he is still legally a married man.

Though the portrait of the Reverend Brede suggests the Reverend Duchemin in *Parade's End* and though George Moffat's good intentions and spirit of self-sacrifice suggest the character of Christopher Tietjens, *The Benefactor* is closer in form to *The Good Soldier*. Both novels, using a four-part structure, develop their stories in a *progression d'effet* by which the story is "carried forward faster and faster and with more and more intensity" to the final effect at the end. However, *The Benefactor* is not an early masterpiece by Ford, for it suffers, as do all of Ford's early novels, by being compared with his true masterpiece, *The Good Soldier*. There is, moreover, a weakness in the portrayal of minor characters, particularly such plot characters as Beale, a caricature of an American go-getter publisher; and Carew, the South American cousin of Clara Brede, who is introduced in the second half of the novel as a self-assured rival suitor in contrast to the hesitant, middle-aged, self-effacing Moffat. There are lapses in style, and the attempt to utilize the symbolic image of the mirror suggests the contrived fire image in *The Shifting of the Fire* rather than the structural images of *The Good Soldier*. And, though the final part of *The Benefactor* progresses more and more intensely to the final scene, there is not the same sense of an inevitable psychological progression from part to part from which the novel gets its unity, as in *The Good Soldier*. The embroilments are not single, for the relationship between Gregory Moffat and his wife remains a separate, contrasting but subsidiary development from the relationship of Clara and George. Their relationships do not form a four-square coterie as in *The Good Soldier*.

The Benefactor should be compared with *The Shifting of the Fire, Romance,* and *The Inheritors* rather than with *The Good Soldier*. In this sense *The Benefactor*, while in itself no masterpiece, is a significant development in Ford's career as a novelist. For the first time he has used the Affair which is the form of his best work; and, though there are flaws in his rendering of it in this novel, it does represent an advance in his mastery of techniques and a surer handling of the love theme in the relationship between George Moffat and Clara Brede, which suggests in a minor key the relationship between Christopher Tietjens and Valentine Wannop in *Some Do Not. . . . The Benefactor* should also be read in comparison with *A Call* (1910), Ford's best novel and his most successful use of the Affair before *The Good Soldier*. But Ford's development as a novelist occurred by twists and turns as he explored different methods and materials, rather than by straight lines. Just as he turned from social satire to a romance in collaboration with Conrad, so he turned from a novel of a small circle to historical fiction, publishing the first novel of his Katharine Howard trilogy the following year, 1906.

II   The Fifth Queen Trilogy

Before he met Conrad and they began their collaboration, Ford had begun work on a biography of Henry VIII, but he never completed it. Undoubtedly, the Katharine Howard trilogy stems from the research on Henry VIII, and perhaps Ford might never have attempted a trilogy on Henry's fifth queen had he not spent time examining the state papers of Henry VIII in the British Museum: "I had got together all my material for the life of Henry VIII and had made a synopsis of the chapters and even a list of illustrations [. . . .] The Book was to be heavily illustrated with reproductions of Holbein and the like" (*Return to Yesterday*, 167-68). In 1905, the year before the publication of the first volume of the trilogy, Ford published a critical monograph on Holbein. And Holbein's famous portrait is the basis of Ford's portrayal of Henry VIII.

Ford follows the broad outlines of history in his trilogy, but he does take considerable liberty with the facts, particularly in his portrait of Katharine Howard. However, a historical novel is essentially fiction, not history; and the manipulation of historical facts may be necessary to achieve artistic or dramatic effects. When Ford most pedantically follows the facts, in over-elaborately explaining the machinations surrounding the court of Henry VIII and his fifth queen, he is least successful artistically. Though he deliberately distorted the true character of Katharine Howard, he did re-create the atmosphere of the times and make the historical personages come alive dramatically. He has, however historically inaccurate, rescued Katharine Howard from the obscurity of history and crowned her a woman of queenly qualities to render the spirit of the age.

Ford's Holbein-like Henry VIII is a lusty king, a heavy eater and drinker, a lustful but faithful lover who is attracted not only to Katharine Howard's fair beauty but also to her Classical training; for he is enough of a humanist to appreciate her command of Latin and the Classics. But he is also a weak-willed man who vacillates between the powerful, opposing forces of his reign, the Catholics and the Protestants; he wants peace in his declining years, foreign and domestic, but he fears loss of foreign influence and domestic power. He is a self-willed man of good intentions, but he is essentially ruled by his passions and moods and has the stubbornness and obstinacy of the self-willed when crossed. Swayed by Katharine, he desires to make his peace with God and with the Pope and agrees to make his submission to Rome. But his motivation is more a fear of death than a deep personal conviction, more a question of affairs of state than of religious principles. He is portrayed as a man caught in the middle of the uncontrollable forces that he himself unleashed in his kingdom, a prey to the machinations of stronger-willed men than he. Thus, Ford's portrait of King Henry VIII is, as Katharine says in her final speech, of "a weak man in very evil and turbulent times."[3]

Though Ford distorts history by minimizing the active role Henry played in pursuing a foreign policy of power politics and a domestic policy of ruthless suppression of opposition to his concept of the king as the supreme head of state and church, this distortion is used for artistic purposes; for Katharine Howard, not Henry, is the protagonist of the trilogy, and Cromwell, not Henry, is her adversary. As Meixner has pointed out, the basic conflict of the trilogy is the claims of God and Caesar; Cromwell, representing the modern totalitarian state, would render unto Caesar while Katharine, representing high virtue and Catholicism, would render unto God. Between them is Henry, "in whose self-doubting personality lies the possibility of either direction."[4]

As we have suggested, it is in the portrait of Katharine Howard that Ford most distorts history. Historians are generally agreed that Katharine was guilty as charged, though it should be noted that she was not specifically charged with adultery. The charge —that she had tainted the royal blood by leading a carnal life before she married Henry, that she had concealed the fact from him, and that she had continued after her marriage to meet secretly with Culpepper and Dearham, with Lady Rochford acting as a go-between—was not only proved but was sufficient to justify the death penalty. Furthermore, in actuality Katharine Howard was not the well-educated woman of great intelligence that Ford portrays, nor was she the strong-willed idealist portrayed in the novel. Indeed, she is described by one historian as a "thoughtless, giddy girl"[5] and by another as a "juvenile delinquent"![6] Historically, it is very doubtful that she much influenced Henry's religious policies since he was more influenced by political considerations in his overtures to Rome than by personal convictions.

However, in the novel the fundamental social, political, and religious conflicts of the time come to a climax at the end of the trilogy in the human drama of Henry and Katharine as husband and wife at the crisis of their relationship. For Katharine, accused of treason, appeals to Henry's love, trust, and belief in her as a faithful wife against all the malicious gossip and charges against her as a woman. She will not defend herself if he does

own high virtue which would admit no compromise with the realities of the time. However, whereas the later tetralogy successfully portrays this, the early trilogy does not. The difficulty lies in the fact that, though we can accept Christopher Tietjens's idealism as the reality of fiction, Katharine's makes a fiction of reality. The pitfall for the novelist of history is that the reader judges his portrayal of historical figures against the facts of history. It is true that the novelist has the right to manipulate historical facts to suit artistic purposes, as Shakespeare did in his historical plays; however, Katharine's idealism and purity are so central to the theme of the novel that the lack of justification in history—indeed, that the reverse is true—makes the whole theme seem based on a false premise.

Paradoxically, Ford's portrait of Henry VIII in relation to Katharine Howard rings true, for from all accounts he was a doting husband and lover and was deeply shocked as a man rather than as a king at the revelation of her immoral behavior of which he had no inkling. Ford ends the trilogy on a deliberate note of ambiguity in their relationship, playing on the ambiguity of the charge against Katharine, that she had conspired to meet secretly with Culpepper but that infidelity with him was not specifically charged: Katharine admits to Henry that she has confessed to the King's Council that Culpepper was her lover, but whether the confession is true or not she refuses to admit. Hers is a small triumph for one who is to be beheaded for being falsely accused, but a fitting punishment for a suspicious husband!

The Fifth Queen trilogy should be read as one novel; but, unlike the tetralogy, there is no elaborate structure of time shifts to achieve a structural relationship between the various volumes. The individual volumes of the trilogy move forward chronologically; the structural pattern is achieved by the movement of the wheel of fortune and by the scenic method. The first volume, *The Fifth Queen* (1906), sees the rise of Katharine even at the moment of Cromwell's triumph in the coming marriage of Anne of Cleves; for Henry is disgusted with the physical appearance of Anne whom he had contracted to marry "sight unseen." Henry becomes enamored of Katharine's fair beauty in contrast to Anne's grossness, and in Henry's infatuation is the seed of Cromwell's downfall since he is too closely linked with the policy that

FORD MADOX FORD

led to the marriage with the Lutheran Anne of Cleves. The
second volume, *Privy Seal* (1907), details the downfall of Cromwell while Katharine ascends and is to become the queen; but
the defeat of Cromwell contains the seeds of her own downfall
because the Lutherans are determined to plot her downfall.
Ironically, the papists themselves who had used her against
Cromwell also reject her, because they would lose their wealth
and power since in her idealism she is determined that the lands
they took from the monasteries must be returned. The final
volume, *The Fifth Queen Crowned* (1908), narrates the defeat
of Katharine who, unlike Anne, is unwilling to compromise her
ideals to save her life.

Ford uses the scenic method in this trilogy more deliberately
and more often than in any other novel aside from *The Good
Soldier* and *Parade's End.* The very historical material lends itself well to the scenic method. The court scenes, the pageantry,
the mob scenes, the private scenes of public figures, the secret
intrigues, the council meetings—all lend themselves to a rapid
alternation of scene. Beyond the historical atmosphere created
by these scenes is the integral part this scenic method plays in
the theme and in the over-all impressionistic technique of the
trilogy. Contrasts of regal splendor and squalid poverty, of high
moral purpose and petty intrigue, of light and dark, of Classical
learning and illiteracy, of summer and winter (to correspond to
Katharine's ascendancy and her downfall), of beauty and ugli-
ness (personified in the contrast between Katharine and Anne),
of rich colors and dark, murky surroundings—all create the impression of a duality of life in this period of transition from the
Middle Ages to the Renaissance.

Set scenes rather than time shifts, as in the various interviews
between Lady Mary and Katharine, are used to suggest an interrelationship between the three volumes and to unify them as a
whole; but at the same time these result in repetition rather than
in development. Certain images are used to reinforce key scenes,
all appearing in the second volume: the butterfly image (Katharine attracted to the power for good of the queenship; Anne
quite willing to get out of it with her life saved, attracted to the
light of material goods and wealth promised her for acquies-
cence); the sunburst image (Henry's marriage to Katharine was
to be the sunburst of his manhood and kingship, as it was to be

for Katharine of her queenship and ideals); and the cat's-cradle game that Katharine and Lady Rochford play (for Katharine was the pawn in the cat's-cradle game of political and religious intrigue).

Ultimately, Ford failed in his attempt to render the history of Henry's fifth queen; as we have already suggested, he is defeated by history itself. But it is not that key minor figures, Lascelles and Throckmorton (whose role in the intrigues and counter-intrigues is pure invention on Ford's part), are disappointingly the stock characters of spy stories, or that the distortions of history, of which there are many, are in themselves the cause. It is that Ford's concept of Katharine's character contains the seeds of its own failure as characterization. Having chosen to render her as the embodiment of high idealism, he cut himself off from her reality as a woman. As the trilogy progresses, she becomes more and more the allegorical representation of ideal queenship, of moral idealism, and of purified Catholicism—and less and less the woman and lover that she was historically. At the end, she does face Henry as wife and woman, but hers is a set speech, pronounced as though from the throne. Yet Ford had succeeded in presenting a sense of the authentic atmosphere of history; and the trilogy—in terms of style, complexity of theme and characterization, and artistic control of technique and structure—represents a significant development in Ford's literary achievement. The trilogy anticipates by many years, both in theme and in the use of the multiple novel form, the tetralogy, *Parade's End.*

III An English Girl

While in the midst of completing the *Fifth Queen* trilogy Ford published a social satire, *An English Girl* (1907), turning again to the contemporary scene as he had in *The Benefactor*. *An English Girl* is an inferior novel which does not give evidence of any significant development in Ford's craftsmanship, but it is of interest at this stage of Ford's early career for what it suggests of later developments. For the first time Ford used the American scene as part of the setting: Ford had visited New York the previous year; and, like Charles Dickens over sixty years before him, he felt that what seemed to characterize America was the noise, the hustle and bustle, the vulgarity of manners, the snooping of

newspaper reporters, and the distortions of the truth in the papers
—if Dickens's *Martin Chuzzlewit* (1843) and Ford's *An English
Girl* can be taken as evidence of an Englishman's first impressions of America.

Ford was to change his impressions of America (in his later
years he spent considerable time in New York), but the attempt
to render the American scene and the American character on the
basis of first impressions suggests the weakness of Ford's approach in this novel: external details and appearances are mistaken for the reality. While awareness of noticeable differences
in dress, manners, and speech may be true to the traveller's immediate response, these superficial differences do not characterize a people. Both Dickens and Ford mistook these differences
as the essence of equalitarianism in contrast to English class
consciousness and manners.

More importantly, Ford viewed the American spirit as a conflict between high idealism and crass materialism with the latter
winning out. Don Kelleg, the American idealist, though he is
more English than American, having been born and educated in
England, is diametrically opposed to his father, who represents
the new kind of wealth typified by the robber baron whose
ideals have been perverted by the doctrines of the law of the
jungle and of the survival of the fittest in the world of business
and finance. Ford's failure in this novel is not in its idea, which
has possibilities as satire and social criticism, but in its conception of character. Don Kelleg as an idealist is so naïve and his
schemes for reform so bookish and vague that the whole novel
takes on the quality of a day dream, "if I had a billion dollars,"
rather than of a serious social satire. This fable-like quality of a
fairy godfather, who dispenses largesse to his fellow man only
to find that his gifts are spurned as charity, vitiates the apparently serious intention of the novel to criticize a materialism
that seeks to justify its evils on the basis of Darwinian theories.

Don Kelleg's father, Charles Collar Kelleg, the great financier
and businessman whose death at the beginning of the novel
makes his idealistic son "the richest citizen in the world," got his
start by robbing his best friend, Kratzenstein, of a mine. But
Kratzenstein refused Don's offer to make amends, asking only
that Don be the man his father was and manipulate the stock
market so that he, Kratzenstein, can make a killing on the worth-

less stocks he owns. Already disillusioned by what he has seen (the slums) and heard (the noise of the elevated trains) in New York and frustrated in giving away money by the terms of his father's will, Don decides to return to the quiet countryside and genteel life of England, only to discover when he returns to England that he really is an American and must go back to do what he can to reform the American spirit.

The subtitle of *An English Girl* is *A Romance*, and the girl of the title is Eleanor Greville, who is engaged to Don Kelleg. That Ford considered this novel essentially a romance suggests its lack of unity, for the different elements of the novel—fable, social satire, comedy, and romance—are never integrated. There is nothing inevitable in the characters' unhappy separation at the end of the novel, when Don decides he must return to America to do his duty and Eleanor decides she must remain in England. Perhaps Ford intended to suggest that the two worlds, the Old and New, can never meet; but the break-up of the romance is artificially contrived to illustrate a theme and does not arise from the psychological and emotional truth of character portrayal. It is true that, from the beginning, it is made clear that Don felt no passion for Eleanor, that she represented for him "a feeling of the Best," and that a rival in the person of her passionate cousin, Augustus Greville, provides a contrast to Kelleg's lack of passion; but the tone of the novel and Eleanor's insistence all through the narrative, that she only desires to do what Don wants, do not prepare the reader for the sudden turn when she will not go with Don because she dislikes America.

An English Girl adds nothing to Ford's development as a novelist. The idealistic-benefactor theme had been handled more successfully in *The Benefactor*. The satiric theme of exploitation and corruption in the financial world he had treated more fully in *The Inheritors*. And the romantic theme in this novel, though quite different, is less successfully developed than either in *Romance* or in *The Fifth Queen* trilogy. Ford was to explore more deeply and complexly the conflict between passion and duty in *A Call* (1910), and he was to portray more successfully and maturely the American businessman in the novel *When the Wicked Man* (1931). But *An English Girl*, for all its weaknesses, does suggest some of Ford's most characteristic concerns—the conflict between social responsibility and personal happiness, the idealistic hero who suffers disillusionment, the sexually passive hero who nonetheless is involved in a romantic situation, and the passionate heroine whose passion is in conflict with her code of behavior.

IV Mr. Apollo

Mr. Apollo (1908), like *An English Girl*, is a social satire; but in narrative form it is much closer to the satirical, scientific fantasy, *The Inheritors*. Its subtitle suggests the fantasy: *A Just Possible Story*; and, as its title implies, the protagonist is the Greek sun god, Phoebus Apollo, who appears on earth in human form to inquire "into the nature of mortal man." Utilizing the satiric device of the utopian tradition, the mysterious stranger who asks fundamental questions about the nature of man and his society, Ford adds a religious dimension to his social satire by making his protagonist an immortal god. For, though there are glimpses of social criticism in the novel, the basic satire is the lack of purpose and faith in modern man's life—whether it be the workingman living in the slum, whose only aspiration is the grave; the Christian missionary, the Reverend Mr. Todd, whose selfish materialism is a perversion of original Christianity; or the press magnate, Lord Aldington, who cares more for the circulation figures of his paper than for the truth.

Apollo's antagonist is Mr. Clarges, the atheist. To him, all priests are charlatans, like the mind-reader Krakroff whom he exposes; and Clarges is determined to expose Apollo as a charlatan since he represents the "most detrimental of all things, Religious Belief." Clarges' militant atheism is contrasted with the skeptical agnosticism (skeptical even of its agnosticism) of his friend, Alfred Milne; and it is for Milne's "soul" that Clarges and Apollo vie. The "battle," however, is one-sided since it is part of the godly nature to be uncaring about whether man believes in God or not. Apollo *knows* he is God, and therefore he does not need man's belief to feed his ego; but man needs Religious Belief or else he aspires only to the grave. Clarges, who represents opposition to all forms of religious belief, hates actively and strenuously.

Science is the new, modern religion; but it offers no final answers and no salvation. Clarges, who refutes scientism, sees science as a threat to individualism and scientists as the priests of the future; science, he charges, has substituted the "open mind" for knowledge, creating new doubts and new mysteries. Catholicism, with its claim to absolute Truth, is presented as an antidote to the open-mindedness of scientism and to the atheism of Clarges; but Carver, an American liberal, refutes the authoritarianism of the Catholic Church, and Apollo asserts that he himself is the Godhead, the one God. Eugene Durham, a rationalist, seeks to find natural explanations for Apollo's mysterious powers; but his explanations are refuted by the miracles that Apollo performs.

Mr. Apollo is a novel of ideas in which the clash of opposing concepts is the essential dramatic conflict. Ford maintained a sufficiently detached control over his material to achieve an artistic balance among the various points of view. It is true that Clarges is presented as a hateful little man, but his arguments are telling. Ford, who himself was a Catholic convert, leaves unanswered the objections of Carver to Roman Catholicism and uses Apollo as his God. It is true that the most severe satiric criticism is leveled at the materialism of modern Protestantism and at its failure to provide moral leadership; but the satire is focused specifically on the selfish and self-centered clergyman, the Reverend Mr. Todd. Mr. Todd is given his chance to be saved, but he is incapable of true reformation: "I have done nothing to be ashamed of, mark that!" are his last words, as he is condemned by Apollo to live the rest of his life as helpless as a baby because he is a priest without faith and a man without hope of reformation.

Contrasted with Todd's living damnation is Milne's conversion. Like Clarges, Milne has been influenced by the ideas of Darwin and Huxley; and he became at first an atheist and then an agnostic. Milne's crisis of belief occurs when all his rationalist ideas come in conflict with evidence of Apollo's godly power to create miracles. As a result of this conflict within him, Milne becomes feverish and is dying. He needs light and air to be saved physically, but the slum buildings and the smoke of modern industrialism block the light of the sun and foul the air. Apollo gives him his chance to be saved spiritually by destroying the buildings (along with the people in them) to let light and air (truth) into his room. Milne is saved; for, through this miracle, he is converted and believes in God.

The weakness of *Mr. Apollo* lies in the conception of Apollo as the symbolic Godhead. One must ask to *what* is Milne converted? Surely not to a cult of modern sun worshippers; that would be farthest from Ford's intention. Perhaps wishing to avoid the difficulty of attempting to portray the Christian God directly, Ford superimposed on a Classical, polytheistic religion a monotheistic concept of God in the portrait of Apollo, thus mythicizing Greek mythology by suggesting that all gods are one God. Milne achieves peace and happiness by believing in Apollo as God, for, as Apollo says, "it is by the worshipping of Gods that men attain to happiness."[7] But, aside from the problem of accepting Apollo as anything more than the traditional literary device of the mysterious stranger who exposes the hypocrisy and foibles of man and society, there remains the weakness of Milne's conversion as a symbolic rather than a dramatic act of human experience; for it is based on the direct evidence of Apollo's supernatural, miracle-making power rather than on a moral crisis and self-knowledge. Todd's damnation, however two-dimensional his character delineation, is more convincingly portrayed because it arises out of his essential nature.

V The "Half Moon" *and* The Portrait

In his next published novel, *The "Half Moon"* (1909), Ford returned to the historical novel, using as the basis for his narrative Jacobean England and the voyage of Henry Hudson in 1609 to the New World to find the Northwest Passage. During this voyage of the *Half Moon*, Hudson discovered and explored the river that bears his name. But, unlike the Katharine Howard trilogy, the central focus of the novel is on the idealistic fictionalized hero, Edward Colman, rather than on Hudson, who, as Wiley points out, "talks like a book" and is portrayed unflatteringly as a bombastic man who uses guile and trickery rather than seamanship (112-13).

The "Half Moon," because of its use of arrests and escapes into the night, its hidden treasure, and its hero being set upon by hired thugs, mutiny on the high seas, seems closer in spirit to an adventure story like *Romance* than to a serious historical novel like the Katharine Howard trilogy. However, the historical material is essential to the theme of the novel. As the subtitle indicates—*A Romance of the Old World and the New*—Ford contrasts the two worlds, England and America. England at this time, though it had emerged from the Dark Ages, is portrayed by Ford as still in the grips of the dark past, as he explains in his dedicatory letter: "there lingered many traces of that darkness; a thousand superstitions, a million old beliefs."[8] And the town of Rye, with its feudalistic privileges gained by the barons in the Middle Ages, is the central focus of that struggle between darkness and light in the Old World. Repressive trade laws, plots against the king and Parliament (the Gunpowder Plot of 1605), oppressions of Puritans and Catholics, superstitious beliefs in witchcraft and black magic, poverty and intolerance—all drove from England the men who were looking for "truths of all kinds: for new faiths, for new methods of government and, perhaps above all, for lands in which Utopias might be found or might be founded" (vi).

Thus the New World was the land of hope. But Henry Hudson is portrayed by Ford as the voyager and discoverer, not as the founder or settler of new lands; he is the Navigator whose dream is the never found Northwest Passage. It is the merchant Edward Colman who envisions a new commercial, utopian settlement on the site of New York where he, killed by Indians, becomes "the first European to die between the shores of the Hudson River" (vii). Colman, ship owner and builder, was a victim of the declining shipping trade during the reign of King James I, who, a man of peace and beset by debts, refused to build up the navy and to use the navy to protect English merchant ships on the high seas; Hudson himself received financial backing for his voyage from the Dutch, not the English. Colman is also the innocent victim of the laws against smuggling (called "owling") to avoid the heavy import duties levied by King James on raw materials, such as wool brought in from overseas. About to be arrested, he escapes only through a ruse (he is eventually pardoned, but only because he is able to buy his pardon through a well established system of bribery).

Like Christopher Tietjens, Edward Colman is victimized by a woman he has spurned, Anne Jeal. The historical theme of two contrasting worlds is integrated with the romantic theme of two contrasting loves: the fair-haired Magdalena Koop whom Colman marries, and the dark-haired Anne Jeal whom Colman re-

jects. Magdalena, daughter of a Puritan clergyman, loves Colman
with a pure heart and soul; her devotion transcends death and
darkness, for hers is a spiritual love that can forgive even the
dark hatred of Anne Jeal's perverted love and can hope to meet
her husband in the "new world" of heaven after the "voyage"
of death. Anne Jeal, mayoress of Rye, loves Colman with a dark
passion that is akin to hate; her love, destructive and evil, is a
selfish one born of vanity and pride, an irrational passion (Colman never encouraged her) that turns readily to hate and cruelty.

Daughter of the Middle Ages, Anne Jeal uses the dark powers
of witchcraft and sorcery to torture and kill her victim. Ford
uses the element of the supernatural in much the same way as
Hawthorne does in *The Scarlet Letter*; he carefully suggests a
natural explanation for every supernatural happening, but the
effect is that the supernatural is real, for both use the historical
setting of a time when people believed in the reality of witchcraft and black magic. Having failed to punish Colman (by
framing him as a smuggler and by having him beaten up by a
couple of hired thugs), Anne Jeal turns to witchcraft as a means
of both punishing Colman and forcing him to come back to her
submissively, his body and will broken. Much attention is given
to the practices of witchcraft, such as the casting of evil spells
and the use of a wax image of the victim; but the thematic intent is implicit in the motivation of the sorceress and in the historical realities of the time: love, whether of God, country, or
man, is not gained by repression and oppression, by superstitions
and intolerance, by poverty and ignorance.

Whether or not one accepts the idea that Colman's death was
"caused" by witchcraft—and Ford deliberately leaves it ambiguous—Colman was in a real sense killed by superstition and
intolerance. Old Jan, one of Hudson's crew, voices the racial
intolerance and superstitions of Europeans toward the Indians:
to him "these peoples and all peoples with black or brown skins
were devils, that was why they had the mark of brownness set
upon them by God" (299). He and others in the crew shoot at
the Indians (who had been converted to Christianity!) and start
the fight in which Colman is killed. Thus the superstition and
the intolerance of the Old World touch the shore of the New
and cause suffering and death. Though the powers of darkness
represented by Anne Jeal's witchcraft are defeated by Mag-

dalena's spiritual love, the darkness of evil lives on in the unregenerate hearts of men. Anne Jeal does not understand at the end why Magdalena should have all and she nothing: "Great God! What was her love to mine that Thou shouldst give her such a strength and render me so weak?" (342). But "by then it had grown quite dark," and she cannot see the light of the truth of her own evil passion. Henry Hudson, maddened with grief at the loss of his friend, accuses the crew of being the cause of Colman's death and says "that the Indians with their clemency were better Christians than they all" (346). But the crew do not understand him; they are Dutch, and he is English; and his interpreter, Edward Colman, is dead.

The Portrait (1910), published the following year, is also a historical romance, but it is a complete contrast to *The "Half Moon."* A late seventeenth-century period piece, it is as light and frothy as the other is dark and serious; comical, at times farcical, it is a surface treatment of the manners and mores of fops and dilettantes. It is an inferior novel not because it is a comedy, but because its basic plot situation is trivial; its historical materials lack any deep or complex thematic significance; and its characters derive from Restoration and eighteenth-cenutry comedy. The rather absurd plot involves the impulsive bet of the wealthy protagonist, Mr. Bettesworth, to find, wed, and house the model of the portrait he himself has not seen (it is vital to the plot that he not see the portrait until the end, for otherwise he would have recognized who it was). In an all's-well-that-ends-well solution, the woman, Lady Eshetsford, whom he loves and for whom he is willing to lose the bet so that he can marry her, turns out to be also the lady of the portrait. Thus he wins the bet and the woman of his heart, an easy solution that the reader suspects all along.

Seemingly authentic in its details, particularly in its architectural details, the historical setting, presumably in the year 1696-1697 during the reign of William III, contains anachronistic references to King George I, Robert Walpole, and Methodism (indeed Bettesworth and Lady Eshetsford are married by a Methodist preacher, Mr. Williams!). It may be that Ford was attempting to show, by telescoping events, that this neo-Classic period, at least in its arts and manners, was a continuum rather than the two separate periods into which history would divide it, the seventeenth and eighteenth centuries. But, if so, the attempt fails, and the allusions remain anachronisms because the historical setting is a surface background rather than an integral part of the romantic theme as in *The "Half Moon."*

Mild satire is provided by the manners and mores of the characters. Farcical duels and near-duels provide a satire on dueling reminiscent of Sheridan's *The Rivals*; country justices are satirized for their provincialism; and aristocratic and wealthy young men about town are satirized for their foppish behavior and dilettantism. The cowardly husband of Lady Eshetsford, Sir John, is derived directly from Vanbrugh's comedy *The Provokéd Wife*, and Bettesworth has a similar role to Constant in the play, for he is constant in his love for Lady Eshetsford. Thus the characters are stock ones from Restoration and eighteenth-century comedy, including the impoverished younger son, Roland, who schemes with his brother's tailor, Boodle, to get money out of Bettesworth who has inherited all the family wealth by accident of earlier birth. But though the characters and situations that are the ingredients of Restoration comedy are found in *The Portrait*, what is lacking is the sparkling wit. Ford was no Oscar Wilde, and his attempts at reproducing the wit and style of the historical period seem merely heavy and derivative.

Ford does interject a more serious note into his novel near the end. Bettesworth, a rather arrogant man of wealth, is humbled and chastened by his experiences in jail where he comes into contact with the seamier side of life that exists underneath the polish and glitter of the upper strata of society but of which he has no inkling. He is temporarily depressed and withdraws from society, but he is offered sugar-coated advice by Lady Eshetsford: "[. . .] take your laurels and wear them, and do not inquire too closely what hand holds the knife that cut them, for I think most great victories are like this, and most great victors, if you could search their hearts are much as you are; for it is nine parts fortune and one of merit, and so the world goes on."[9] If Ford intended to suggest a more serious historical theme—that underneath the glittering exterior of wealth there was great suffering, poverty, and injustice which remained hidden—it is too tenuously suggested. The final emphasis is essentially that of romantic comedy, for all's well that ends well.

VI   A Call

With *A Call* (1910) Ford returned to a treatment of the Affair first developed in *The Benefactor*. Though *A Call* appeared the same year as *The Portrait*, its publication actually preceded the latter by a few months since it appeared serially in the *English Review* the previous year. But, since *The "Half Moon"* and *The Portrait* are both historical romances and provide a revealing contrast in Ford's approach to the genre of the historical novel, it is fitting and logical that they should be considered together rather than be separated chronologically by a discussion of *A Call*. For Ford's development as a novelist leading to *The Good Soldier* and to *Parade's End* should be viewed not entirely as a straight chronological line; one must also take into consideration the type of novel he was writing. Thus *A Call* can be seen in relation to the earlier novel, *The Benefactor*, as a development of Ford's approach to the novel of "small circles" leading to its culmination in *The Good Soldier*.

A Call looks forward to *The Good Soldier* because of a considerable development in the artistic control of the elements of the Affair from *The Benefactor*. As in *The Good Soldier*, there is intense concentration on the entangled lives of the characters (five in this instance) who dance their highly civilized dance of ritualized sexuality: "It appeared to him [Robert Grimshaw, the protagonist] that they were going ironically through a set of lancers [. . . .]"[10] The lancer, a quadrille, like the minuet in *The Good Soldier*, is a controlling symbol in the novel; for, as Meixner has pointed out, "like the dance, the action of the novel evolves through a set of variations, until the pattern of opposed desires with which the book was begun is at the end ironically reversed" (136).

The basic plot situation is disarmingly simple: Dudley Leicester, recently married to Pauline Lucas, accidentally meets his former love, the dark-haired, passionate Etta Stackpole (now Lady Hudson), while he is alone in London, and spends the night with her. While he is with Etta, they are interrupted by a phone call from someone who recognizes his voice but whom Dudley does not recognize. Driven literally mad, Dudley fastens his tormented mind on who the caller was and what he might do. Out of such seemingly thin narrative material Ford wove an

intricate web of entanglement in the lives of his characters, for
Dudley's one act of infidelity affects all the other characters
whose lives are already embroiled with his. Dudley's marriage to
Pauline was managed by his best friend, Robert Grimshaw, who
loved Pauline but who felt committed to marry Katya Lassarides,
if he married anyone, even though their engagement had been
broken some years before. Thus Grimshaw seeks to share in
Pauline's life through Dudley, without sacrificing a vague sense
of honor and duty to remain faithful to Katya who still loves
him, but who refuses to marry him. Katya refuses to marry him
although she is willing to become his mistress; but he will have
her only if she agrees to marry him.

The subtitle, *A Tale of Two Passions*, most obviously refers
to Grimshaw's love for both Pauline and Katya; but the set of
lancers involves different combinations of the dancers, including
the complex relationship between Grimshaw and Leicester.
Though never explicit, there is a definite suggestion of latent
homosexuality in Grimshaw's relationship with Leicester: a self-
effacing man, regular in his habits, middle-aged before his time,
a seemingly confirmed bachelor, Robert Grimshaw takes Dudley
Leicester under his wing, straightens out his estate, turns him
into a model landlord, and marries him to the woman he himself
loves. What seems to be a natural interest in his best friend's
affairs is motivated by an unnatural desire to marry Pauline
Lucas by proxy through Leicester, thus enjoying her love without physical passion. Reminded by his aunt of his early youth,
when he would stand for minutes at a time watching the garden-
er's six-year old daughter, he says,

That's what I want in Pauline. I don't want to touch her. I want to
watch her going through the lancers with that little mouth just open,
and the little hand just holding out her skirt, and a little, tender expression of joy. [. . .] When I was that boy it didn't occur to me that
I could have Katya; we were like brother and sister, so I wanted to
watch little Millie Neil. Now I know I might have Katya and I can't,
so I want to watch Pauline Leicester. I want to; I want to; I want
to (16-17).

At the same time, hidden beneath the surface of his passionless existence, is a dark passion that has no outlet. Like Christopher Tietjens, who is described as an elephant, Grimshaw's

appearance is that of a slightly ridiculous man—"that chap is like a seal" are the first words spoken of him in the novel—who advises women on where to buy their dresses and who is likened to his dog Peter, a dachshund who is patient, gentle, and obedient. Grimshaw states the theme that becomes more fully developed in *The Good Soldier*: "We haven't learned wisdom: we've only learned how to behave. We cannot avoid tragedies" (274). But underneath the exterior of polite behavior is suppressed passion; he offers a bunch of violets as a wedding gift to Pauline, which she bitterly throws at his feet. His attempt to love Pauline from a distance by merely watching her results in their drifting toward an illicit passion that neither of them dares to fulfill: Pauline, out of loyalty to Leicester; Grimshaw, out of guilt for his meddling. In a moment of self-revelation at the end, Grimshaw says, "I'm only a meddler who muddles and spoils. That's the moral of the whole thing" (290). In wanting to share Pauline with Leicester, he has managed to muddle the lives of all involved; and, as a result, he has shared in the guilt of Leicester's infidelity. For it is revealed, through the use of time shift, that Grimshaw himself was the mysterious caller.

In a sense, Dudley Leicester is Robert Grimshaw's double, a motif Ford also uses in *The Good Soldier* to illuminate the relationship between Dowell and Ashburnham. Although this motif is never made explicit in *A Call*, it underlies their whole relationship: Grimshaw married Pauline by proxy through Leicester, but Grimshaw also betrayed his love for Pauline by turning her over to another man while he maintained the appearance of an honorable man loyal to his duty. Leicester does what Grimshaw subconsciously would like to do, but which his code of behavior would not allow—commit adultery. However, his sense of guilt drives Leicester mad, and Grimshaw, motivated by jealousy, is the instrument of Dudley's terrible punishment. Furthermore, Dudley's "two passions" are a reflection of Grimshaw's own: the dark passion for Pauline, which he will not allow himself; and the dutiful passion for Katya, which his code of behavior will neither let him give up or attain illicitly. Thus, as Pauline points out, he ruins all their lives.

Like Leonora Ashburnham in *The Good Soldier*, Pauline remains loyal to her husband; it is part "of our day and our class" not to make a scandal even though she really loves Grimshaw.

Anticipating the terrible irony of Dowell's relationship with Nancy Rufford in *The Good Soldier*, Pauline becomes the caretaker of her husband who, though he looks like "a picture of ox-like health," is seriously ill with fear and guilt. He is unable to cope with the consequences of his act of passion, just as Grimshaw was unable to cope with his two conflicting passions. It is Katya who triumphs in the end; Grimshaw surrenders to her and agrees to live with her on her terms. But, having triumphed, she decides to marry him—a decision which ironically would have avoided all the tragedy if it had been made at the beginning. But, unlike *The Good Soldier*, *A Call* ends hopefully if not happily: Dudley will eventually be cured of his madness by Katya, just as she cured her niece Kitty of an anxiety neurosis which manifested itself in the same way by a refusal to talk.

A Call is Ford's best novel before *The Good Soldier*. The early novels—of history, of romance, of social satire—are uneven in quality; for Ford did not always achieve artistic control over his materials in these types. That Ford alternated between these different kinds of narrative material tends to obscure the fact that his most characteristic techniques—impressionism, *progression d'effet*, indirect rendering of emotions, symbolism, time-shift, and the scenic method—are best suited to the novels of small circles. Therefore, if one considers the development of Ford's mastery over these techniques in relation to the narrative materials from *The Benefactor* to *A Call* and then to *The Good Soldier* (each published five years apart), one sees more closely the movement or development of Ford's craftsmanship toward what Wiley calls "the perfected affair," achieved in *The Good Soldier*.

The technical accomplishment of *A Call* points directly toward the achievement of *The Good Soldier*: the entangled lives of the five characters are emotionally embroiled in a single, unifying "affair" that progresses more and more intensely to its culmination in Katya's victory, symbolized by Grimshaw's gesture of surrender: "his hands fell desolately open at his side." The scenic method, which Ford learned from James and from Conrad, but which is also inherent in the impressionistic technique, is used effectively to probe the various psychological and thematic aspects of the affair not only through dialogue, but also indirectly through significant details of the setting and gestures of the characters. Symbols, such as the lancers and Grimshaw's dog Peter, are used to suggest a pattern in the lives of the characters that Ford saw in life itself: "I don't mean that of birth, apogee, and death, but a woven symbolism of its own" (*Return to Yesterday*, 204).

Yet *A Call* is not the "perfected affair" that *The Good Soldier* is, even though it is richer in theme and in technical accomplishment than any of Ford's previous novels. The main weakness of the novel is in the portrayal of Dudley Leicester, whose madness is central to the theme of the novel. Leicester is not a fully realized character and the obvious device of the telephone call looms too large as the single focus for his psychological and moral guilt; his relationship with Etta Hudson, both past and present, which is the basis for the anxieties that lead to his madness, is not sufficiently developed to balance the parallel "two passions" of Robert Grimshaw.

Related to this inadequacy of character development is the technical flaw of the time-shift used near the end to reveal Grimshaw as the one who made the phone call. While the suspense does provide an inkling into Leicester's character—that he focuses his fears on the identity of the caller and not on the moral implications of his act—more is lost than gained in keeping this vital information from the reader through most of the novel. The element of surprise, which Ford states that he and Conrad agreed was "the one quality that gave interest to Art" (*Conrad*, 189), was sometimes taken too literally by Ford; and the surprising revelation is viewed by the reader as a contrived trick rather than as a valid artistic quality. Moreover, because Grimshaw's revelation as the caller is delayed until nearly the end of the novel, the psychological and moral aspects of his meddling are insufficiently explored in relation to Leicester's madness; for what matters is not that the mystery of the call should be solved but that it was Grimshaw and not a stranger who made it, with all its implications of complex motivations and character revelation. In *The Good Soldier* Ford mastered the device of suspense without sacrificing either credibility of plot or depth of character portrayal and thematic material. Indeed, he probes more complexly into the relationship of the past event to the present situation—with its discrepancy between appearance and reality—through the narrator's consciousness.

VII   The Simple Life Limited

The Simple Life Limited (1911) is an anti-utopian novel, satirizing in particular the good life in the form of an utopian, self-sufficient, Socialist community dedicated to "Beauty, Religion, Art, Poetry itself, and all the Finer Things," as envisioned by William Morris and Leo Tolstoy. Vegetarianism, Fabian Socialism, pre-Raphaelite medievalism, equalitarianism, estheticism, individualism—all are satirized through the various characters who represent and expound these ideas. The Simple Lifers, enslaved by the logic of an abstract ideal, are ridiculed for the absurdity of their complicated, impractical solutions to the simple, practical problems of everyday living. For example, their medievalist, craft-oriented concept of life dictates that they should not use machines made by machines; therefore, bicycles are banned in the community and walking is encouraged, but nothing made of animal matter may be worn (since animals are fellow creatures). And thus sandals must be made of vegetable matter, even though they fall apart; and clothes must be made of it, even though they do not keep out the rain and look like prison uniforms. Thus the "simple life" of these people is more complicated and tangled, more rigidly doctrinaire and conventional, more hypocritically a sham and a fraud, than the society it seeks to reform.

The title of the novel suggests the main focus of the satire: the simple life—as practiced by its founder, Mr. Gubb, a disciple of William Morris; and by its principal pamphleteer, Mr. Bransdon, a poet and novelist—is so narrowly limited in its vision that it is neither simple nor good, neither beautiful nor true, neither poetic nor free. Mr. Bransdon, who gave up writing novels to write absurd pamphlets on the evils of wearing corsets and leather boots, symbolizes in his present indolence the lack of vitality and creativity of the whole community. "Free" ideas have so enslaved the minds of the colonists and their leaders that unconventionality of behavior and of belief is valued for its own sake. Hamnet Gubb and Ophelia Bransdon (their very names suggest the absurdity of their "tragedy") marry in a purely conventional ceremony but for presumably unconventional reasons—it is a passionless "union of reason" for the utilitarian purpose of promoting the cause of the Simple Life, he being the son of the founder and she the daughter of its present leader. But their main "defiance" of the conventions is that they take her family's name rather than his because it sounds more beautiful! Their respective fathers react like conventional Victorian fathers to the news of the marriage, but for unconventional reasons—Hamnet is really Bransdon's illegitimate son—and thus the hypocrisy of Gubb and of Bransdon is exposed.

The title also suggests another aspect of the satire, one which is a devastating stroke of irony. The title can also be taken as the title of a business concern, for the Simple Life is a paying proposition. What emerges from all the details of eccentric behavior, of radical ideas, and of slum conditions is that all are tolerated by the gentry because the settlement pays a dividend of eight and a half per cent to the stockholders. Mr. Gubb's shrewd business sense has made a sound, capitalistic enterprise out of a Socialist scheme; and, as Lady Croydon says, if the Simple Life Limited shows a profit, then "there's nothing the matter with its morals."[11] Mr. Gubb is feted at the end by the gentry not because of his Socialist ideas but because he is a successful entrepreneur; and, though the colony is destroyed by fire, Mr. Gubb moves on to another such enterprise, the East Croydon Garden City Ltd.

Mr. Bransdon shakes off his lethargy, a manifestation of his disgust with himself and the colony, and returns to reality. Pointing to the villagers, a "sombre, ugly group of human beings," he says, "that is the Simple Life!" (371). Thus, the true life, for all its weaknesses and flaws, is a normal existence in society. But his son Hamnet, an individualist to the end, goes into the woods to live his version of the simple life, an English Thoreau, observing nature to be one with Nature, living life as it comes with no rules, seeking to become an "artist in Life." In contrast, Ophelia seeks happiness in society, marries the stage manager Everard, and becomes a socialite. All these resolutions of the characters' lives are hastily told in the final chapter; a conventional ending, tying up loose ends and carrying the characters' lives into the future, it tends to dissipate some of the satiric impact of the novel because the resolutions are made too easily.

Contrasted to the absurdities of the Simple Lifers is the mild-mannered, kindly, compassionate, Tory landlord, Gerald Luscombe. By no means an idealized character—there is doubt as to the legitimacy of his birth, he has led an unhappy youth, and his marriage to a woman of fashion and modern taste is not ideally suited to his sedentary habits and Classical scholarship— Luscombe is nonetheless a sane, commonsensical contrast to the wild, nonsensical eccentricities of the Simple Lifers. His life is complicated, but it is fruitful in maturity of wisdom and richness of passion as contrasted with the unnecessary complications and foolish ways of the Simple Lifers.

As a Tory landlord, he is kinder to his tenants than Socialist Gubb, whose profits depend on the slave labor of the colonists and on the slum conditions of the living quarters. As a Classical scholar and yet a physically active man, Luscombe is a contrast to the sluggish, apathetic Bransdon, who no longer believes in what he has written (the enduring Classics are themselves a contrast to the ephemeral tracts Bransdon has put out). Yet Luscombe is something of a social exile; he has deliberately shunned the gentry of the county because he is not sympathetic with their bourgeois values even though, like them, he is a Tory landowner. His values are the outmoded ones of the old benevolent landlord, and the others are closer in outlook to the hypocritical materialism of Mr. Gubb.

The Simple Life Limited is a more successful satire than *Mr. Apollo*. The characters, given the nature of the satire, are necessarily ridiculous, even at times grotesque (for example, the mad Brandetski goes berserk over love for Ophelia, sets fire to the cottages, and then kills himself). But within the framework of the allegorical intention of the character portrayals, Ford has provided a delightful gallery of eccentric character types ranging from the pre-Raphaelite artist of the colony, Miss Egmont, who paints allegories of the simple life out of corsetless ladies, doves, butterflies, roses, halos, and poetic inscriptions, to the ridiculous literary critic Mr. Parmont and the cynical theater director Mr. Everard. Except for the epilogue, the satire is sharper, more comic, and more sustained than Ford had achieved up to this point.

VIII   Ladies Whose Bright Eyes

An important and constantly recurring theme in Ford's novels is the chivalric ideal of honor as embodied in the English concept of a gentleman.[12] From George Moffat's benevolence in *The*

Benefactor to Gerald Luscombe's sense of kindness and decency, Ford evolved a type of character, a modern man of honor, which culminates in the portrait of Christopher Tietjens in *Parade's End*. In Ford's next novel, *Ladies Whose Bright Eyes* (1911), the chivalric ideal is presented literally. Using the same device of fantasy that Mark Twain employed in *A Connecticut Yankee in King Arthur's Court*, that of transporting a modern man back into the Middle Ages, Ford presents an opposite view of chivalric ideals. To Mark Twain, the knights were nothing more than reactionary enemies of progress, "a band of slaveholders under another name." To Ford, the ideal of honor is embodied in the code of chivalry.

William Sorrell, a book publisher, is knocked unconscious in a railway accident just after he has been given the Tamworth-Egerton crucifix as collateral for a loan by Mrs. Lee-Egerton. The suggested magical properties of this holy relic and the *dopplegänger* legend that the soul of an unconscious person may enter the body of another (a device Ford uses again in the late novel, *The Rash Act*) are the means by which Sorrell is transported back to the fourteenth century. Much of the first part of the novel is taken up with detailing life in this era and in convincing Sorrell that he really is "in the middle of the Middle Ages" and not in the midst of an elaborate pageant reconstructing the "days of yore." That he may be the victim of a hoax is a cumbersome device of suspense, but it does serve the purpose of contrasting his modern attitudes with the gradually evolving influence on him of the chivalric ideal. As a modern man Sorrell's innate sense of decency has been corrupted by the idea of material progress symbolized by the airplane: like Mark Twain's Connecticut Yankee, Hank Morgan, he is tempted by the sense of power his modern knowledge gives him over the people of the Dark Ages. With his knowledge, he declares, he could make Lady Blanche de Coucy the Empress of the World—he could "invent" the airplane and terrorize every city in the world; they could burn Paris down in a night.

But, when Lady Blanche—who represents the attraction of the dark forces to man, her bright eyes "alight with the contagion of enthusiasm"—suggests that then he shall be her emperor, Sorrell immediately refuses because she is already married and one must not do anything dishonorable or scandalous. This contradiction between public and private morality is modern man's dilemma between the idea of material progress, which finds its justification in the nineteenth-century concept of survival of the fittest, and a code of personal ethics which is traced back to the chivalric ideal of knightly honor. When Sorrell falls in love with the fair Lady Dionissia de Egerton, he has also fallen in love with the fourteenth century; and he no longer wishes to destroy its values.

Ford's rendering of the historical period is authentic in details; but, though he does not judge it harshly as Mark Twain did, neither does he sentimentalize or idealize. In *The Simple Life Limited*, published the same year, Ford satirized the pre-Raphaelite idealizing of the Middle Ages and humorously and ironically referred to himself as an author esteemed by the Simple Lifers as an authority on life in that period. Ford presents ample details of the grim, hard, unsanitary lives of the people in the "good old days"; and he is critical of the clergy in his portrayal of the malicious gossip of the Mother Abbess and of the materialism of the Dean of Salisbury Cathedral.

The aristocrats are portrayed as living, loving, and warring in sharp contrasts of luxury and filth, illicit romance and loveless marriages of convenience, valor and cowardice. But what stands out for Sorrell as a positive value amid the squalor and harshness of the Dark Ages is the *public* ideal of honor typified by the knightly code of chivalry, which in modern times can only be found in the *private* ethics of a few individuals. Sorrell is knighted in the fourteenth century for his good work and his valor (although his valor is actually the better part of indiscretion). He is knighted in the twentieth century for publishing encyclopedias, a measure of the adulteration of the chivalric ideal; for Sorrell, originally a mining engineer, viewed publishing as just another business to manage, the product to be engineered to the tastes of the public and not sanctified as Art and Literature.

When Sorell "returns" to the twentieth century, he finds it ugly and worthless; but he is still under the romantic spell of the fourteenth century and his love for Lady Dionissia. Through his nurse, Dionissia Morane, a reincarnation of his romantic dream, he discovers (or rediscovers) love and hope; and he learns the lesson from her that one century is just as good, and just as bad, as another, and that "Romance [. . .] is the flavour of any time."[13] Sir William Sorrell and the nurse-healer Dionissia Morane marry and live happily ever after in their rebuilt fourteenth-century castle with all the modern conveniences, including plumbing, electricity, and garages. They possess the best of two possible worlds.

The ending is wholly unsatisfactory in its sentimental resolution of Sorrell's discovery of love for what he cannot really possess—a fourteenth-century way of life and a fourteenth-century lady. It only makes ridiculous Sorrell's whole experience of the Middle Ages that the only monument he can leave to the reality of his dream is to rebuild his dream castle. While *Ladies Whose Bright Eyes* is not an uncritical defense of the Middle Ages, it does suggest the serious theme that something more important and valuable has been lost along the way than the gray stone walls of a castle which can be rebuilt, something more significant than the lack of sanitation and light which modern plumbing and electricity can correct. What has been lost, the reader has been led to believe, is a code of honor as a way of life. Yet the reader is left with the easy moral that one century is as good or as bad as another, invalidating the contrast between Sorrell's twentieth-century and the fourteenth-century mind, and that love is where you find it, for love is a mystery that "makes all the ages one," and thus Lady Dionissia and Dionissia Morane are one and the same.

Ford, dissatisfied with this original ending, drastically revised it in 1935. Though the healing power of Nurse Dionissia's love is retained, the romantic theme is more integrated with the historical theme: the site of the old castle is to become symbolically enough an air station, and thus Sorrell's sentimental hope of reconstructing the past is destroyed by the reality of technological progress. Instead, he and Dionissia will leave England and make a new beginning in the Russian Caucasus where Sorrell had once worked as a mining engineer. Though this is also an easy solution to a complex problem of psychological and sociological reconstruction, Ford seems to have used, as Meixner suggests, the belief current in the 1930's that the Soviet Union represented a new faith and a new beginning; it is a symbol, however, rather than an ideological conviction (74-75). Thematically, at least, the change is more consistent with Sorrell's experience than rebuilding a fourteenth-century castle.

IX The Panel

Like *The Portrait, The Panel* (1912; published with minor revisions in the United States the following year under the title, *Ring for Nancy*) is a light, frothy comedy; but it is set in modern times rather than in the late seventeenth century. Subtitled *A Sheer Comedy, The Panel* is a comic treatment of a romantic theme Ford has presented more seriously elsewhere, notably in *A Call*. It is the theme of the honorable young man who is really in love with another woman, but who feels duty bound to marry the woman to whom he is engaged. Major Edward Brent Foster is engaged to marry Olympia Peabody, a proper Bostonian; but he is really in love with Nancy Savylle whom he has despaired of marrying because she is now Lady Savylle. Lady Savylle, disguised as the maid Nancy Jenkins, maneuvers Olympia into rejecting the Major through a series of farcical bedroom situations in which a secret sliding door (called "The Panel") plays a prominent part. In the end, of course, Major Brent Foster is to marry Lady Savylle, and the surprise revelation is not that Nancy Jenkins reveals herself as Lady Savylle, but that the Major reveals that he knew it all along.

What rescues this novel from being the frivolous book Ford half-seriously, half-mockingly apologizes for in his dedicatory letter is its delightfully satiric comedy on literary tastes. Major Brent Foster is the youngest man to gain that rank in the army, and he achieved it by reading all of Henry James and trying to understand every line; the effort "toughened his brain fibre" so that he passed his officer's examination brilliantly, but it also ruined his eyes so that he was no longer fit for active service. In a parody of the Jamesian style, the Major is fond of saying, "So that there we all, in a manner of speaking, are." But, as he explains, one can never make out where "they" are; therefore, it is "strengthening to the brain to work it out." The Major attempts to create a demand for James's novels by asking for them at the bookstalls, but no one has heard of him, and the intellectuals never buy novels, but wait for them to be discarded by the lending libraries. Set off against the satire on Henry James and his readers is the more devastating satire on popular romantic, erotic fiction written by such as Mrs. Kerr Howe who mistook the Major's polite attention for romantic adventure. She is considered by the bookstall manager to be the greatest writer the world has ever seen because her works have enjoyed a sale of seventeen and a half million copies, which if stacked on their sides would reach from the earth to the moon, and if laid end to end would reach twice from the earth to the moon and back.

More obvious is the satire on puritanical Bostonians: Olympia Peabody is honorary secretary of the Massachusetts Reformatory and Perpetual Grand Mistress of the Boston Society for the Abolition of Vice. She seeks to amalgamate the society for the Abolition of Vice with the London Society for the Suppression of Sin headed by Mrs. Foster, but Mrs. Foster, president of the society for social reasons, really believes that her nephew the Major should sow his wild oats before settling down to marry Olympia. Her husband is president of the Society for the Reform of the Stage, and Flossie Delamare, the musical comedy actress and former love of the Major, is seeking Mr. Foster's backing for a new theater. The satire on popular taste is climaxed by the fact that Mrs. Kerr Howe seeks to write plays for the new theater; they star Flossie, who is proud of being "the symphonic embodiment of quaint imbecility." Thus *The Panel*, while not particularly noteworthy in its romantic theme, is enjoyable in its comic, satiric thrusts. Obviously Ford enjoyed writing in a relaxed comic mood. As he writes to Miss Ada Potter in his dedication, "I suppose, in this odd, frequently unpleasant and almost always too serious world, even a person so earnest as yourself feels the desire to be made to laugh by an historian so obviously earnest as I am."

X   The New Humpty-Dumpty

The New Humpty-Dumpty (1912) is the weakest of the three satires Ford published within a three-year period (*The Simple Life Limited* and *Mr. Fleight* being the other two). It is burdened with an improbable plot involving the devious, behind-the-scenes machinations of a counter-revolutionary organization that seeks to restore the monarchy in the fictional South European Republic of Galizia. The counter-revolution succeeds in what would appear to be a satirical parody of a comic, bloodless revolution except that the reader is expected to accept the idea that a monarchy is inherently benevolent and a republic inherently corrupt.

Ford does succeed in portraying satirically the materialistic motivations of those who financially back the counter-revolution as a business investment. Counterpointed against the materialism of the others is the idealism of Count Macdonald who unselfishly seeks "to retain for the world something that the world already possessed" but was fast losing through the complexity of the machine age: the happiness of an agrarian and craft-oriented Simple Life. Pitted against the warm light of the simple life (and Galizia is bathed in sunlight) is the dark forest of the heart. Mr. Pett, whose utopian theories of the simple life Macdonald seeks to put into practice in Galizia, destroys him out of petty jealousy. Though remorseful for his pettiness, Pett is satirized as the intellectual who is emotionally immature and morally weak; and he contrasts to Macdonald who represents the chivalrous gentleman of good breeding and lineage, acting unselfishly out of a sense of duty and decency. Death itself is an act of unselfishness; he insists with his dying breath that his murderer be let free and that his death be attributed to natural causes so that the new king will not be faced with the scandal and crisis of a trial on the very day of his restoration. Echoing Clara Brede's protest against George Moffat's ideal of self-sacrifice at the end of *The Benefactor*, Lady Emily Aldington comments in anguish on Macdonald's dying act of selflessness: "Ah! always the other first."[14]

An inferior novel, *The New Humpty-Dumpty* is nonetheless of particular interest to the student of Ford Madox Ford because it anticipates in its theme *The Good Soldier* and in its character types *Parade's End*. The epigraph to *The New Humpty-Dumpty* directly states one of the major themes of *The Good Soldier*: "There be summer queens and dukes of a day,/But the heart of another is a dark forest." The theme of the dark forest of the heart is stated again and again in the novel, and Macdonald's last words are, "The dark forest! The dear dark Forest!" Indeed, Ford states in the dedicatory letter that he originally had entitled it "The Dark Forest," but the publisher, John Lane, insisted on its present title. However, Ford does not achieve in this novel the complexity of theme revealed in *The Good Soldier*, and the recurring statement of the epigraph becomes repetitious rather than, as in *The Good Soldier*, a deepening journey into the dark forest of another's heart.

The darkest forest is the heart of the Countess, Macdonald's wife. A prototype of Sylvia Tietjens in *Parade's End*, the Countess is, like Anne Jeal in *The "Half Moon,"* a madly jealous woman bent on destroying the man she loves. She is unable and unwilling to release him to another woman partly because of sexual possessiveness and partly because of a perverted sexuality that is gratified by torturing the man she loves. The reader can accept the malignant vindictiveness of Anne Jeal because of her witchcraft, but the extent of the Countess' hate, a vitriolic hate so literal that she intended to throw a glass of vitriol in the Count's face, is without adequate explanation either in the inherent necessity of the situation or in the emotional logic of human motivation.

Because he is more credibly portrayed, the Count Macdonald more nearly represents a prototype for Christopher Tietjens than the Countess does for Sylvia Tietjens. A man of honor, an idealist, a gentleman, Count Macdonald is Ford's latest portrait of the modern chivalric hero. Like Christopher Tietjens, Macdonald's chivalry is vilified because it is seen as a sign of weakness and as a confirmation of guilt; his willingness to act decently in his wife's suit for separation is unheard of in legal circles, and his desire to be generous to his wife only infuriates her more. The discrepancy between the appearances of his behavior and the reality contribute to his downfall, as it does for Christopher Tietjens, since appearances are taken as reality; and it appears as though Macdonald is simultaneously carrying on an affair with Lady Aldington and keeping a prostitute in his rooms.

In contrast to the Countess is Lady Emily Aldington, suggesting the contrasting pair in *Parade's End*, Sylvia Tietjens and Valentine Wannop. Lady Aldington, Ford's portrait of an ideal woman, implicitly trusts Macdonald and asks only "to be certain of his goodness of heart." She shares his idealism and his belief in honor and duty, and she fears only his fate: that the very selflessness that she loves will ruin him. And it is his inability to recognize "the wolves" that exist in the dark forest of another's heart that is his undoing; on the very day of his marriage to Lady Aldington, having honorably obtained his divorce from the Countess, he is murdered.

Mr. Pett, the intellectual, who himself would never commit an act of violence, had implanted the idea of murder in others, and

Macdonald is killed by an assassin who had taken Mr. Pett at his word. Thus, like Magdalena in *The "Half Moon,"* Lady Aldington loses her husband to the dark forces of the world. But though Macdonald dies, his idealism lives on in the young king who is restored to the monarchy. Humpty-Dumpty is put together again, and Macdonald's chivalric ideal is reborn in the king who will carry out Macdonald's idea of utopia, a place where there is light, not darkness, in the hearts of men. The theme of rebirth in a place of sun and light anticipates the theme of reconstruction in the healing sun of Provence found both in the autobiographical *No Enemy* (1929) and in the late novel *Henry for Hugh* (1934).

XI Mr. Fleight

Like *The New Humpty-Dumpty, Mr. Fleight* (1913) is a political satire; but it treats directly and specifically the corruption and Machiavellism involved in English party politics. Basically, the story is that of Mr. Aaron Rothwell Fleight, a wealthy but socially unknown Jew, who wants to do something and be somebody in politics. He approaches the cynical but influential Mr. Blood, who agrees it can be done at the cost of "£150,000 a year for sheer bribery." The rest of the novel details the machinations by which Mr. Fleight's candidacy is advanced, including backing a literary magazine "to advertise you to thinking people," indirect bribing of voters, contributing to the party coffers, and getting "an expensive wife for the social side of things." But Mr. Fleight only wins the election accidentally, for his opponent dies suddenly during the campaign and Mr. Fleight is left unopposed.

Mr. Fleight nearly lost the election because of his sentimental principles. Mr. Blood suggests that it does not matter which party he chooses because both are corrupt, but, since he is running as a Radical, Mr. Fleight wants to learn how the working class lives and to share his wealth with the poor. As a result of his sentimental attachment to the simple life, he causes the suicide of Gilda Leroy, who believed in the romantic fairy tale learned from novels and thought that Mr. Fleight was a fairy prince come to marry her. The resulting scandal would have lost him the election except that his opponent dies just after the nominations are closed. When Fleight is elected, he also wins the woman he loves, Augusta Macphail, who will marry him only if he has succeeded.

Mr. Blood is the antithesis of Mr. Fleight. Too cynical to believe in party principles (he is a Radical but also a large, wealthy landowner), he provides a satirical commentary on the state of politics in modern times. Too lazy to do anything himself, he is motivated by his cynicism to sponsor Mr. Fleight's political career as a practical experiment in Machiavellism, "so that it might amuse me," and at the same time to help the careers of his young friends, Mr. Mitchell and the Misses Macphail, who want to publish a literary magazine of their own.

Blood's bitterness at "the dirty comedy of life" and at society as a "cruel and disordered machine" is inadequately motivated. He had years before—the reader is informed, as the "justification" for his cynicism and self-exile from society—strangled his groom in Newport, Rhode Island, for doping his race horses; but the killing was all hushed up by the influential aristocrats who were behind the horse-doping. While undoubtedly the affair was a disillusioning experience for the young Mr. Blood, there is something other than idealism involved in Blood's strangling the groom who sold the ideals of loyalty, faithful service, and devotion for a thousand dollars; there is involved a feudalistic, class-conscious concept of life that would justify the killing of a servant who has been disloyal. This class-consciousness is seen also in Blood's criticism of Fleight's wanting to live among the lower classes as a disaster because classes should not mix socially. Intended as a satire on wealthy Radical politicians with social consciences, these criticisms betray a Tory bias in all of Mr. Blood's supposed Radical politics.

The Tories, one must hasten to add, are satirized unmercifully also. The pompous Chancellor of the Exchequer, Parment, is disconcerting to the Conservatives because of his democratic views; but these are so vague that the only advice he can give to young politicians like Debenham is to "cultivate idealism." Parment's idealism, only apparently the opposite of Blood's cynicism, is satirized as being merely an unwillingness to notice the corrupt practices of politics; and Debenham, who is disgusted with Blood's cynical views of politics, learns nothing from one of the most powerful men in his own party. Gregory, Fleight's Tory opponent, is an incompetent "stick" who has been chosen to run for the seat vacated by his fellow party member, Mr. Cronk. Mr. Cronk has had to leave the country because of illegal stock manipulations; the Tories hope to win by bribing the voters at the cost of five pounds a head. But the voters themselves are the main object of the satire, for their willingness to be bribed and their stupidity as voters are the underlying causes of corruption in politics.

The literary satire is focused on the *New Review*, the *avant-garde* magazine backed by Mr. Fleight to advance his candidacy among the intellectuals, and on the Enamel Club, a kind of pre-Raphaelite group dedicated to the ancient Chinese art of enameling on copper. The *New Review* is edited by Charlie Mitchell, who assembles a wonderful collection of cranks, "and, of course, it's cranks that get a thing a reputation in the intellectual world"; but it is the hard-working, practical assistant editor, Augusta Macphail, who makes the magazine a success. The Enamel Club, an odd collection of eccentrics and social climbers, is presided over by the Swinburne-like, esthete poet, Mr. Cluny Macpherson, who recites his own bad poetry at the drop of a rhyme in a loud, high-pitched voice that drives people away. Macpherson is more gossip than poet, and it is for this gossip that he is tolerated; it is he who spreads the story of Fleight's connection with Gilda Leroy, and thus nearly loses the election for Fleight.

However, though Ford attempts to link the two worlds, the literary and the political, they remain separate centers of satirical interest and separate vehicles for its satirical barbs. What Ford did achieve in *Mr. Fleight* was a multiple satire of the Edwardian Age; the politically ambitious have their counterparts in the literary and social worlds where cant, hypocrisy, and avarice rule. The political parasite, Garstein, who sells the Byefleet candidacy to Fleight, has his counterpart in Macpherson, who "sells" his gossip for a chance to read his poetry; the politically ambitious Reginald Debenham has his counterpart in the socially ambitious mistress of Mr. Fleight, a vulgar Cockney girl who has appropriated the title of Baroness di Sonnino and who is a counterpart not only to the practical Augusta Macphail, whose ambition is to marry a successful politician, but to the romantic Gilda Leroy, who sees life as a Cinderella story.

As a counterpoint to all the ridiculous types—whether political, social or literary—Ford sets Mr. Blood's younger brother, Reginald, who is portrayed as a "gentleman of great ability," a mathematician and engineer whose early career was blighted by a ridiculous divorce scandal that made him a public laughingstock. As a result, he had a nervous breakdown and retired from public life; but he is now ready to return to active life in politics, and his brother will back him against Mr. Fleight, whose political naïveté is contrasted with Reginald's knowledge of the ins and outs of practical politics. Unfortunately, as a character Reginald Blood is a pale shadow in the background of his brother's more dominant personality; and he does not provide the needed balance in the novel. Blood's cynicism remains the dominant, controlling intelligence of the novel.

XII The Young Lovell

The Young Lovell (1913), an otherwise inferior historical romance, is of interest in the development of Ford's treatment of the chivalric ideal. *The Young Lovell* is set in the fifteenth century at the beginning of Henry VII's reign, when the breakdown of the feudal powers of the nobility and the beginning of the modern age took place. Historically, the barons, greatly depleted in ranks during the civil war and the feuding of the past hundred years, were opposed to any assertion of central authority by the king because they feared the loss of their feudal rights. Even though Henry VII, a Lancastrian, had married Elizabeth, daughter of Edward IV, a Yorkist, the Yorkists opposed him and plotted against him. Lord Lovell, a friend of the Yorkist king, Richard III, attempted to kidnap Henry VII in 1486; and this failing, he and other Yorkists hired an impostor who claimed to be the Earl of Warwick, the Yorkist heir to the throne. Henry defeated these forces in the Battle of Stoke in 1487.

Ford distorted the historical facts to enhance the romantic element and to develop the chivalric theme. Instead of the plot against the king, Ford uses the impostor in a plot against Young Lovell, legitimate heir of Lovell Castle; Decies of the South (whose name suggests a pun on the word deceit) wishes to dispossess Lovell of both his inheritance and his wife. Decies, the illegitimate son of Lord Lovell (his mother was supposedly a witch who disguised herself as a nun, and thus his conception is doubly damned), disguises himself as the Young Lovell and is wedded to Lady Margaret in Lovell's place. Lord Lovell literally dies laughing at the deception (Decies was his favorite, suggesting his alliance with the forces of evil in the world); and Decies takes possession of the castle.

Young Lovell, an ideal Christian knight, is nonetheless tempted by the sensual life represented by the supernatural vision of the White Lady; this tempting vision, which holds him for ninety days, delays him and enables Decies to take over the castle and falsely accuse him of the sin of sorcery. Eventually Lovell storms the castle and defeats Decies. However, believing himself to be guilty of sensuality, though not by deed, Lovell denies himself the fruits of victory and becomes a holy hermit. He does penance for the rest of his life because he considers himself unworthy of the chivalric ideal of being a "soldier of Christ and Our Lady" (in contrast to Decies who made a mockery of the whole ceremony, symbolizing the lack of true faith in the chivalric ideal, the religious rite being a mere formal ritual to him). But the final irony is revealed: Lovell does not really do penance; conforming only to the outward forms of the holy hermit's life, in his mind he dwells in an imaginary valley with his White Lady, enjoying "the gentle pleasures of love."

Thus *The Young Lovell* is more a moral parable than a historical novel. Using the outward trappings of history—the feuding nobles, the conflict between the barons and Henry VII, the conflict between Church and State which came to a climax during the reign of Henry VIII—Ford seems to suggest that the chivalric ideal of honor and duty was lost not only by outward corruption, but also by inward thoughts of infidelity to the ideal. The sensuous life of the nobility, the machinations of the court, the feuding of the nobles, and indeed the supposed origins of Decies—all contribute to the breakdown of the code of chivalry.

However, though Young Lovell is innocent of the public charge of sorcery against him, he is guilty of wanting to share in that corrupt life, a desire which immobilizes him at the beginning so that the evil forces under Decies can be unleashed, and which makes him incapable at the end of assuming the duties and responsibilities of his knighthood. Lovell represses his sensual desires, but in so doing he becomes guilty of mentally indulging them and of neglecting his duties while the world looks on and marvels at the good soldier of Christ. This suppression of sensuality which leads to a tragic separation of mind and body, and of appearance and reality, becomes the basis of Ford's penetrating psychological and moral study of modern man in his next novel, the masterpiece, *The Good Soldier.*

CHAPTER 3

"My Great Auk's Egg":
The Good Soldier

THE *donnée* for *The Good Soldier* is to be found in *The Spirit of the People* (1907), Ford's impressionistic study of England and the English. In it is the "true story" of a married man who fell in love with his young ward, until, when "the situation had grown impossible," the girl was sent on a trip around the world to save the marriage and prevent scandal. Ford was asked by the husband, who was "afraid of a 'scene,'" to accompany them to the station; but the parting was so lacking in display of tenderness or any emotion, without so much as a goodby, that it seemed "to be a manifestation of a national characteristic that is almost appalling." The girl died en route at Brindisi, and Ford comments "that at the moment of separation a word or two might have saved the girl's life and the man's misery without infringing eternal verities."[1] From this anecdote, like James's *donnée* for *The Spoils of Poynton*, Ford fashioned *The Good Soldier*, a masterpiece so closely interwoven in theme, character, structure, and technique that it reaches Flaubert's ideal of the perfect fusion of form and subject matter: "The Idea exists only by virtue of its form."

I *Method of Narration*

The Good Soldier is divided into four parts; while this structural division is not unusual in the conventional narrative, *The Good Soldier* does not progress chronologically. Rather, Ford relies upon *progression d'effet*, a theory of narrative progression developed by Ford and Conrad during their collaboration: "in writing a novel we agreed that every word set on paper [. . .] must carry the story forward and, that as the story progressed, the story must be carried forward faster and faster and with more and more intensity" (*Conrad*, 210). Partly, this theory is the logical extension of Poe's theory of the short story; partly, it is based on Flaubert's concern with style in relation to subject and form. But what is unique is the idea that the story must be carried forward faster and more intensely as it progresses. *Progression d'effet* is best exemplified in Conrad's work by *Heart of Darkness,* in which Marlow (and his listeners, and, by extension, the reader) journeys more and more deeply into "the heart of darkness," penetrating at a faster and more intense pace into the psychological and moral darkness of man's evil self. It is best exemplified in Ford's work by *The Good Soldier* in which John Dowell (and his listener, and, by extension, the reader) unfolds, layer after layer, the surface manners of these "good people," penetrating at a faster and more intense pace to the psychological and moral core of rottenness.

Crucial to the control of the narrative is the role of the narrator, John Dowell. As his name suggests, Dowell holds the story together, linking the various parts and giving unity to the whole. Through his mind we "know" the others; through his *impressions* we "see" the events and relationships revealed in the novel. The choice of narrator is therefore essential to the rendering of impressions, and Ford chose a narrator who is centrally involved in the situation. Although Edward Ashburnham is the protagonist of the "story," Ford has created a novel with a double focus, just as Conrad utilized Kurtz and Marlow in *Heart of Darkness.* And indeed Dowell eventually identifies himself with Ashburnham (just as Conrad explores the double self in "The Secret Sharer," so does Ford in his later novels, *The Last Post, The Rash Act* and *Henry for Hugh).* The effect is quite similar to James's use of the governess as the narrator of *The Turn of the Screw,* for like Dowell's, it is her psychological and moral impressions of appearances and realities which are the central focus of the novel.

The "occasion" for the novel is Dowell's "telling" the story to an imaginary sympathetic listener some months after the suicide of Edward Ashburnham. As Dowell states at the beginning of Part Four, he is telling

[. . .] the story as it comes. And, when one discusses an affair—a long, sad affair—one goes back, one goes forward. One remembers points that one has forgotten and one explains them all the more minutely since one recognizes that one has forgotten to mention them in their proper places, and that one may have given, by omitting them, a false impression. I console myself with thinking that this is a real story and that, after all, real stories are probably told best in the way a person telling a story would tell them. They will then seem most real.[2]

Thus the past is reconstructed not as a chronological report of what happened from beginning to end, but as a series of impressions as they are remembered and relived in the mind of the narrator. The intent of the narrator is to re-create for his listener the immediate experience of the event or scene, tempered, however, by the irony of present knowledge and re-examined in the light of later knowledge.

This going back and forward over the affair necessitates a manipulation of time sequences as though the story were being told "in a very rambling way so that it may be difficult for anyone to find his path through what may be a sort of maze" (183). Yet *The Good Soldier* is anything but rambling; it has its own inner logic and order of time, as does Faulkner's *The Sound and the Fury*. The progression of the novel is, as Ford defined this "New Form" of the novel,

[. . .] the rendering of an Affair: of one embroilment, one set of embarrassments, one human coil, one psychological progression. From this the Novel got its Unity. No doubt it might have its caesura—or even several; but these must be brought about by temperamental pauses, markings of time when the treatment called for them. But the whole novel was to be an exhaustion of aspects, was to proceed to one culmination, to reveal once and for all, in the last sentence, or the penultimate [. . .] the psychological significance of the whole. (Of course, you might have what is called in music your Coda.) (*Thus to Revisit*, 44).

The narrative pattern of *The Good Soldier*, that path through the maze, is suggested by two controlling images—the first stated at the beginning of the novel, and the second at the end—"four-square coterie" and "shuttlecocks." The unity of the Affair, its oneness of embroilment and psychological progression, is suggested by the intimate cohesiveness of the group that excludes the outside world and by the group's appearance as a solid front of friendship that is permanent and stable. More importantly, the image of the four-square coterie suggests the various possible combinations of relationships among the four that are revealed

as the novel progresses—Edward and Florence as lovers, Florence
and Leonora as antagonists, Edward and John as rivals for Nancy
yet in the end as alter egos, Leonora's love-hate of Edward that
alternates between attraction and repulsion, paralleled by John's
love-hate of Leonora—to say nothing of the fact that the Dowells
and the Ashburnhams are on the surface seemingly happily married couples presenting to the public eye a solid front of friendship. The four-square coterie image alternates between suggesting a "stepping minuet," with all its implications of a graceful
way of life that is dead, and "a prison full of screaming hysterics,"
just as the novel itself shuttles between keeping up appearances
and giving way to hysteria.

Each of the four parts examines and re-examines different
facets of the interrelationships of the two couples and the various
individuals, like Maisie and Nancy, who are drawn into the center of the square by one or the other of the four. The focus of
the novel shifts back and forth among the coterie like a shuttle-
cock as light is shed on an individual or on a relationship. The
pattern is not haphazard: as a character or relationship is illuminated in a scene, light is thrown on all the other characters
because of the interlocking unity of the group. It may be nothing
more than Florence's laying her finger on Edward's wrist (Chapter Four, Part One), but it is sufficient to involve and reveal all
four of them. Thus the novel progresses at a faster and more intense pace as each aspect contributes to the psychological significance of the whole, culminating in the final revelation. The
listener-reader is drawn deeper and deeper into the labyrinthine
way until the heart of darkness is reached and the heart of the
matter is known: the core of rottenness in man.

II Time

The very rhythm of The Good Soldier with its alternations of
mood and tempo (its progression and caesura) moves like parallel lines "more and more swiftly to the inevitable logic of the
end."[3] Time is not measured by the calendar or the clock as
though events were categorically separated and unrelated in
space and time. Ford's historical sense, his sense of the past,
achieved in the historical novels, is here applied to his sense of
the present: events, though they may *appear* to be so at the time

they occur, are not isolated happenings unrelated to the past or the future. Thus the date, August 4th, is not merely a day on the calendar of the year 1874, 1899, 1900, 1901, 1904, or 1913; the dates, respectively, are those of Florence's birth, of her trip around the world, of her affair with Jimmy, of her marriage to Dowell, of the death of Maisie Maidan and the beginning of Florence's affair with Edward, and of Florence's suicide. The date is a living link with the past, a revelation of the present, and a portent for the future. It is an important and structural symbol in the novel.

At eleven o'clock on the night of August 4, 1914, as every English schoolboy knows, England declared war on Germany. At approximately the same hour on the night of August 4, 1913, as every reader of *The Good Soldier* knows, Florence Dowell committed suicide. It is principally by this device of the fateful date that Ford links the microcosm of his fictional characters with the macrocosm of a world at war, thereby enlarging the scope and significance of the novel. For what the novel explores are the causes of failure in human relationships, whether it be in love, marriage, friendship, national character, or international relations. The events leading up to Florence's suicide and Nancy Rufford's madness six months later are the causes of the breakdown of civilization, of a world gone suicidal and mad.

There are some discrepancies in references to dates in the novel, particularly in the sequence of events that occurred during the first four days of August, 1904. For example, the first meeting of the Ashburnhams and the Dowells at the watering spa of Nauheim, the trip to the castle at M—where Leonora learns that Florence is Edward's mistress, the boxing of Maisie's ears by Leonora which Florence witnesses, and the death of Maisie occur early in August and all but the first specifically on August 4th. But Dowell later states that Maisie's death occurred a month after the two couples had met, which would put the latter event early in July not August. In the manuscript version of *The Good Soldier* Ford changed the date of the first meeting of the two couples from July, 1906 to August, 1904. Dowell's later statement would be consistent with the original July date, but apparently Ford did not catch the discrepancy in relation to Dowell's statement when he changed the date in the manuscript.[4]

However, the larger pattern of narrative time in the novel is unaffected by the minor factual discrepancies, for the time sequences are consistent both with the theme and with the psychological progression of the novel. Narrative time in *The Good Soldier* is not merely a realistic, chronological account of events as they happened; for *The Good Soldier* is an impressionistic novel, not a naturalistic one. Time is rendered through the impressions and memories of the narrating consciousness of John Dowell, who is not an omniscient narrator. A Bergsonian account of "lived time," it is intensive, qualitative, intuitive, indivisible; it is a concept of time and memory in which the living past merges into the present.[5]

Thus, the memory of the narrator does not "lapse"; the "truth" of his recollections is not sequential factualism but psychological impressionism leading to a comprehension of the past by the telescoping of events. Indeed, Ford *deliberately*, through his narrator, focuses attention on the "facts" of time so that the careful reader will realize that what is important is not calendar or clock time, but the psychological and symbolic interrelationships of events. The events reported as all having happened during the first four days of August, 1904, are one indivisible continuum of interlocking memory in the mind of Dowell, having, according to Bergson, an immanent existence in one's consciousness along with an awareness of the present moment.

Thus also, the Anglo-American world generally considers August 4, 1914, when England declared war on Germany, as the date for the beginning of World War I. But in actuality Austria declared war on Serbia on July 28th, thus beginning a series of interlocking events. A series of mobilization orders and ultimatums between Russia and Germany occurred from July 29th to August 1st, and Germany declared war on Russia on August 1st. France mobilized on that day; Germany on August 3rd declared war on France and invaded Belgium on the morning of August 4th, with England's declaration of war the result.

These fast-moving events, all interrelated and dependent on one another, were a continuum of crises in the historical sense; and in the psychological sense they could be telescoped into the action of one symbolic day. Similarly, Ford telescopes the events of August 4, 1904, and crowds the fateful day of August 4, 1913, with a similar series of crises—Ashburnham's romance with Nancy Rufford begins, Dowell learns his wife once had an affair with

Jimmy, and Florence commits suicide. The macrocosm of a world at war is thus symbolically linked to the microcosm of the private world of the characters in crisis, and both are moving more and more rapidly toward catastrophe and the end of the world as they knew it.

The whole novel is structured, therefore, around the August 4th date. Although the exact date is first specifically mentioned at the beginning of Part Two, Part One narrates or refers directly or indirectly to all the important interrelated events connected with this date (the only exception being Florence's affair with Jimmy, which occurred on August 4, 1900). Part One ends with the death of Maisie on August 4, 1904. Part Two begins with a specific summary of the date as a portent in Florence's life and ends with the events of the night of August 4, 1913. Part Three begins with the revelation to Dowell of his wife's infidelity with Ashburnham (begun on or just before August 4, 1904; ended August 4, 1913) and of the reasons for her suicide, and it ends with a summary of Ashburnham's series of loves up to the death of Maisie and the taking on of Florence (which "caused" Maisie's death). Part Four reveals the consequences of Florence's suicide on that portentous date: it leads ultimately to Edward Ashburnham's suicide and to Nancy Rufford's madness. The interlocking events which are the cause of Florence's and Edward's suicide and Nancy's madness are like the events that led to World War I —each move caused a counter move because of the entangled embroilment of the nations and their alliances; each action of the characters caused a reaction in the others because of their entangled lives.[6]

III   *Central Idea*

The Good Soldier, in spite of its title, is not a "war" novel in the sense that Hemingway's *A Farewell to Arms* and Remarque's *All Quiet on the Western Front* are, nor even in the sense that Ford's *Parade's End* is. Nor is *The Good Soldier* an allegory about the defects of society traced back to the defects of human nature as Golding's *Lord of the Flies* is. Yet *The Good Soldier* is a "war" novel in that it analyzes the seeds of destruction in human nature and, by extension, in human society on the verge of war; and it is an allegorical novel in that society is made up of types like the Ashburnhams and the Dowells, the "good people" who rule the nation and guide its destiny, and, with all the good (and bad) intentions in the world, bring it to ruin and disaster. The *rationale* of the novel is to reveal the process by which this happens.

This *rationale* is explicitly stated in the first chapter:

> You may well ask why I write. And yet my reasons are quite many. For it is not unusual in human beings who have witnessed the sack of a city or the falling to pieces of a people to desire to set down what they have witnessed for the benefit of unknown heirs or of generations infinitely remote; or, if you please, just to get the sight out of their heads.
>
> Someone has said the death of a mouse from cancer is the whole sack of Rome by the Goths, and I swear to you that the breaking up of our little four-square coterie was such another unthinkable event (5).

Thus, the break-up of the four-square coterie is the break-up of civilization itself, heading toward disaster. Though the dissolution of the intimate group seems to occur suddenly through a series of crises and catastrophes (suggesting the days of feverish diplomatic negotiations after the assassination of Archduke Ferdinand in the summer of 1914 and the crisis days of August 1st through 4th), the novel's main concern is with the causes of the break-up. Therefore, the emphasis in the novel is on the ironic discrepancy between the coterie's outward appearance of permanence and stability and the inner reality of its being cancerous from the start, just as cancer may fester for years and then break out with painful and mortal suddenness.

Yet the discrepancy between appearance and reality is a double irony, for if the minuet image is false, then the whole of life, manners, and morality are false and the proper man is "a raging stallion forever neighing after his neighbour's womenkind" (12). If man is nothing more than a beast, then war is his destiny; and all that man has achieved in civilized behavior is "a folly and a mockery." Dowell shrinks away from accepting such a conclusion: "For, if for me we were four people with the same tastes, with the same desires, acting—or, no not acting—sitting there and there unanimously, isn't that the truth? If for nine years I have possessed a goodly apple that is rotten at the core and discover its rottenness only in nine years and six months less four days, isn't it true to say that for nine years I possessed a goodly apple?" (7).

However, by the end of the novel the reader can accept no other conclusion; for he comes to discover, as Dowell had discovered, that the very virtues of civilization are the cause of its downfall. Just as Swift strips away the appearance of man's pretense to Reason, so Ford penetrates deeper into the "dark forest" of the human heart to reveal the core of rottenness hidden from view. It is a small consolation to man to realize that his "goodly apple" was good only because he was ignorant of its rottenness. It is indeed "the saddest story" because the tragedy is that "it is all a darkness."

The rottenness at the core is a disease of the heart. This sickness of heart is similar to E. M. Forster's theme of the undeveloped heart in *Passage to India*: "For it is not that the Englishman can't feel—it is that he is afraid to feel. He has been taught at his public school that feeling is bad form. . . . He must bottle up his emotions, or let them out only on a very special occasion."[7] However, Ford emphasizes much more than Forster the "cold" heart that is symbolized by Florence's locked bedroom door (and obversely by Leonora's door that is always open) and that is represented most obviously by Dowell's own lack of passion. Edward's passion is perverted into sentimentalism; Leonora's, into hate and martyrdom. All of them, however, keep up appearances of happiness; it is good form to do so.

The technique Ford employs in developing his theme of the heart is similar to Thomas Mann's use of physical disease or deformity as a symbol or symptom of spiritual sickness, except that in *The Good Soldier* even the physical disease itself is a sham and thus part of the moral rottenness. This literal deception of the heart, carried on by both Florence and Edward (with Leonora's tacit acceptance), is a corollary of the main theme: "this pitch of civilization to which we have attained, after all the preachings of all the moralists, and all the teachings of all the mothers to all the daughters *in saeculum saeculorum*" (10) has amounted to nothing more than a mere morality of manners by which true immorality is hidden by appearances in order to avoid scandal. It is underlined by the fact that Maisie Maidan, the only truly innocent character in the novel, is the one who really suffers from serious heart trouble and who actually dies of heart failure; and yet the suggestion seems to be that she is able to preserve her innocence only because the disease is real.

At the beginning of the novel the reader learns that Florence "had, as the saying is, a 'heart'" (4). One is led to believe, as Dowell himself was, that she died of heart trouble. The irony here lies not in the fact that the reader is deceived by the narrator (the purpose obviously is that the listener-reader must be deceived in order to understand Dowell's shock of recognition that appearances are a deception), but that in a figurative sense Florence died of a "broken heart" when she learned Edward no longer loved her. Yet even the "broken heart" is not the final "truth"; what ultimately drove her to suicide was not the loss of Edward's love—she might have tried to win him back—but that the truth of her earlier infidelity with Jimmy was now known and she could no longer hope to retain her public image of a respectable married woman or to continue to deceive her husband. The true sickness of her heart was vanity.

Dowell also reveals at the beginning that "Captain Ashburnham also had a heart" (4). Dowell (and the reader) learns that this is the story told to dispel any possible scandal involving Edward's leaving India to follow Maisie (49). Even Florence's father supposedly "had a heart," but he died of bronchitis at the ripe old age of eighty-four. Although there was nothing physically wrong with his heart, he spent his life guarding against his heart, suggesting that Florence's supposed heart trouble was hereditary. Significantly, Dowell inherits Mr. Hurlbird's fortune through Florence.

If Florence lacks heart, she does not lack passion. But Dowell does, at least until the end, when he falls hopelessly in love with Nancy. It is not that he did not "love" his wife (they even manage to elope romantically), but that Dowell, being a proper Philadelphia gentleman, did not respond to her one gesture of passion toward him the night of their elopement. Though Dowell is truly deceived by his wife's "heart," it nonetheless suits his passive personality to play the part of a male nurse. And Dowell's role as nurse, related as it is to the theme of the sick heart, is a key to the primary theme of the novel, for the dark forest of the heart, the core of the rottenness, is this disease of the heart which creates an evil not only out of basic human drives, but also out of the subtler morality of manners.

If Edward and Florence commit adultery, they do so, therefore, out of love and passion; if Leonora tortures Edward and drives him to suicide, she does it out of hate and jealousy; but Dowell's intellectual detachment and analytical observation are a subtler form of evil. In accepting his role as nurse to Florence, he must accept the responsibility for creating a "shock-proof world," for heading "off what the English call 'things'—off love, poverty, crime, religion, and the rest of it" (16). In other words, Dowell must create a rarefied atmosphere that denies life itself. Dowell's tragedy, then, is his lack of commitment to life itself; in a moment of self-revelation near the end of Part One, he recognizes that he deserves neither heaven nor hell—"perhaps they will find me an elevator to run" (71), an appropriately modern reward for one of the living dead.

The ultimate significance of Dowell's role as nurse is not revealed until near the end of the novel when, acting as nurse to Nancy, he says: "So here I am very much where I started thirteen years ago. I am the attendant, not the husband, of a beautiful girl, who pays no attention to me" (236). Caretaker of a sick world gone mad, he is unable to minister to it because, as he reveals at the beginning, "I know nothing—nothing in the world —of the hearts of men. I only know that I am alone—horribly alone" (7). He has experienced nothing; he has felt nothing; he "has nothing whatever to show for it" (36). Ultimately, his is the greater evil; for he has denied life itself.[8]

The Ashburnhams (and the Dowells) are "what in England it is the custom to call 'quite good people'" (4). This categorization is a recurring statement throughout the novel and is essential to our understanding of the relationship of the microcosm of the novel's "affair" to the macrocosm of the world at large. With all its implications of governing class, of Anglo-Saxon tradition, of refinement of manners and morals, and of cultural heritage and the comfortable material life, these "good people" represent the best that civilization has to offer. Thus, the rottenness at the core of their lives is the rottenness of Anglo-American civilization, and the end of that four-square coterie is the end of that civilization itself.

Related to the concept of the "good people" is the idea of "the good soldier." Though Ford states in his dedicatory letter that he suggested the title "in hasty irony" and "never ceased to regret

it" (xxi), the title is suggestive of its theme. Edward Ashburnham is obviously the good soldier. In a literal sense, he is "a
first-rate soldier," but also in a larger sense he is the good soldier
of civilian life—he "was the cleanest-looking sort of chap; an
excellent magistrate [. . .] one of the best landlords [. . .] a pains-
taking guardian" of the poor and of drunks (11). He was, in a
word, a sentimentalist, "for all good soldiers are sentimentalists
—all good soldiers of that type" (26-27).

The irony of this appellation is revealed by Dowell immediately: "he was just exactly the sort of chap that you could have
trusted your wife with. And I trusted mine—and it was madness"
(11). And, as though Ashburnham really believed it, "he would
say that constancy was the finest of the virtues. He said it very
stiffly, of course, but still as if the statement admitted of no
doubt" (27). In his sentimentality, he really did believe it. The
emptiness of good form—of the appearance of courage, loyalty,
honor, constancy—as opposed to the reality of being courageous,
loyal, honorable, and constant, is the essence of his sentimentality
and good soldiery. He believed intensely and optimistically "that
the woman he was making love to at the moment was the one he
was destined, at last, to be eternally constant to" (27-28). The
details of his self-deception are revealed in the rest of the novel,
particularly in the last two parts. Yet even at the end when he
faces up to himself, as any good soldier should, his honor is
destructive of self and of others. In the best of good form, he
quietly says goodby to Dowell, as though he were about to take
a nap before tea; and he goes to cut his throat in the privacy of
his room.

The climax of Part One (Chapter Four) illuminates the relationship between Florence and Leonora, but it also sheds indirect
light on the relationship between Florence and Edward and that
between Leonora and Edward. At Florence's insistence they all
view the pencil draft of Luther's Protest. Looking into Edward's
eyes, Florence says,

"It's because of that piece of paper that you're honest, sober, in-
dustrious, provident, and clean-lived. If it weren't for that piece of
paper you'd be like the Irish or the Italians or the Poles, but particularly the Irish. . . ."

And she laid one finger upon Captain Ashburnham's wrist (44).

Leonora, reacting violently to the scene, says to Dowell: "don't you see what's going on?" But when Dowell, though he instinctively suspects the truth, denies he knows, Leonora backs away from breaking up the coterie and instead refers to Luther's Protest: "Don't you see that's the cause of the whole miserable affair; of the whole sorrow of the world? And of the eternal damnation of you and me and them . . ." (45).

Ironically, Leonora's failure to inform Dowell of the true significance of Florence's laying of her finger on Edward's wrist illuminates one aspect of the macrocosm—man's inability to live in harmony and peace with his fellow man. Florence's militant Protestantism and Leonora's narrow Catholicism clash as abstract ideologies. Yet the reverberations of the clash illuminate the personalities involved in the reflected light of this scene. Dowell, passive and uncommitted to life, is relieved to understand it intellectually as a clash of ideas that is kept impersonal by Leonora because of Florence's "heart." Even Leonora withdraws from her vision of hell and becomes "just Mrs. Ashburnham again." Yet, as Dowell realizes later, Leonora's Catholicism is the key to her personality and particularly to her relationship with her husband as a philanderer. Florence's triumphant Protestantism is a reflection of her conquest of Edward; the finger on Edward's wrist is her victorious gesture that lets Leonora know that she has conquered Edward. Florence knows at the same time that Leonora, because of her Catholic sense of martyrdom and because Florence is supposedly a "heart" case, will do nothing overt.

Parts One, Two, and Four all end with a death scene; significantly, Part Three begins with a detailed description of Florence's death and ends implicitly with the theme of the death of the heart, Leonora's. The end of Edward's affair with Maisie was to be, according to Leonora's plan, the beginning of her again winning Edward's love. Though Leonora could not know that Maisie would die as she did, she took comfort in the fact that this affair had to be passionless because of Maisie's heart condition. But "Florence knocked all that on the head." Furthermore, one of the reasons Florence committed suicide was that Edward was already beginning his romance with Nancy Rufford; thus, all of Leonora's hopes, all of her reasons for waiting while Edward went through his "rutting season," were false to begin with. The minuet becomes a dance of death though all the formalities of that graceful dance are maintained: Leonora "had been drilled—in her tradition, in her upbringing—to keep her mouth shut" (177). The death-wish is strong in all four of the coterie; but Leonora survives because of her Catholicism and because she enters into a normal marriage after the death of Edward. Dowell survives because he has been dead, emotionless and passionless, all along. As Dowell himself says, he must "get back into contact with life. I had been kept for twelve years in a rarefied atmosphere" (122).

The death of Maisie is that of innocence; not only is she innocent (her attack is brought on by the shock of realization that Leonora has brought her to Nauheim so that Edward can make love to her), but her death is also the beginning of nine years of deception by the other three. It is only Dowell's ignorance that makes those years happy ones. The happiness itself was true; what was false was its basis. The suicide of Florence "knocked all that on the head" too. And, with the suicide of Edward about four months later, the whole edifice, the "safe castle" that seemed so permanent and stable, crumbles.

IV *Color Symbolism*

Color symbolism is an important corollary to the theme of heart. Whereas heart and passion are associated with red, pink is associated with the dilution, or, at least, suppression of emotions. When Dowell learns that Florence's death was a suicide, he remembers only the *pink* effulgence from the electric lights in the hotel lounge. When Edward receives Nancy's telegram, printed on *pink* paper, that she is having "a rattling good time" on her trip, he reads it without showing a trace of emotion and hands it to Dowell without a word. Then he goes quietly to his room and cuts his throat with a pen knife (one might imagine the *red* effluence of blood, but it is the only death in the novel that occurs "off-stage." Maisie, though she dies grotesquely with the lid of the portmanteau closing over her head, is quickly arranged by Leonora to look like "a bride in the sunlight of the mortuary candles." Florence's body is "quite respectably arranged" on the bed as though she had died peacefully).

Though Edward, pink-complexioned, displays no outward emotion on receiving the pink-paper telegram, his inner emotions are in turmoil; for the telegram is a double shock to him—in his sentimentality, he would have expected Nancy to suffer as he does; and in his heart he recognizes Leonora's triumph in separating Nancy from him. Only good form keeps him from showing his despair in front of Dowell, just as he brought Dowell along with him to the train station to see Nancy off in order to prevent "a scene": "There was upon those people's faces no expression of any kind whatever. The signal for the train's departure was a very bright *red*; that is about as passionate a statement as I can get into that scene" (250, Italics mine).

Ashburnham *does* act, even if his act is one of self-destruction. Dowell, however, on learning of his wife's death, "felt no sorrow, no desire for action, no inclination to go upstairs and fall upon the body of my wife" (108). True, he too has received a shock: he has just learned that Florence had an affair with Jimmy before their marriage. But the truth is that his whole life has been a pinkish effulgence—not without feeling, in fact he is too much the man of sensibility, but without deep emotions or significant actions. He identifies himself with Edward at the end, which provides the novel with its double focus; but he himself admits he is the fainter image (revealingly, Edward talks to him as though he were "a woman or a solicitor"): "I loved Edward Ashburnham [. . .] because he was just myself. If I had had the courage and the virility and possibly also the physique of Edward Ashburnham I should [. . .] have done much what he did." Significantly, of course, Dowell does not do what Ashburnham did, for he lacks those very qualities of Ashburnham. It is the good form that makes Edward seem like Dowell; what is the appearance of respectability in Ashburnham is the actuality of Dowell's personality. As Dowell admits of himself, "I am able to assure you that I am a strictly respectable person. I have never done anything that the most anxious mother of a daughter or the most careful dean of a cathedral would object to. I have only followed, faintly, and in my unconscious desires, Edward Ashburnham" (237).

Florence, Edward, and Leonora all have blue eyes, and both Florence and Leonora wear blue to heighten the blueness of the eyes. It is not objectivity but impenetrability that is symbolized by the blue eyes; the eyes alternate between expressing cold defiance and warm tenderness, yet neither coldness nor tenderness is the ultimate truth of these "windows of the soul"; but, like the waters of the blue sea, they only reflect the surface. Dowell's first sight of Ashburnham is that his face typified English unemotionalism: "There was in it neither joy nor despair; neither hope nor fear; neither boredom nor satisfaction" (25). And Florence hides her face in her hands, Dowell's last sight of her alone.

Significantly, Edward's complexion (and Florence's and Leonora's) is smooth and clear, symbolizing the smooth, clear surface of their lives, apparently unmarked by any deep emotion. Leonora's one emotional outburst that results in overt action, the boxing of Maisie's ears, is smoothed over by the social lie that the small gold key suspended from her wrist had tangled in Maisie's hair. This is the key to her dispatch case which she keeps locked and in which, Dowell suggests, Leonora perhaps "locked up her heart and her feelings" (32). Florence kept her bedroom door locked (the first time Dowell entered her bedroom was the night she died), and behind it she hid her heart and feelings. Leonora kept her door wide open, but only to hear "the approaching footsteps of ruin and disaster"; the first time in nine years she entered her husband's bedroom was to tell him she would divorce him so that he can marry Nancy, offering herself in a martyrdom that her church forbade. For nine years they hide from the rest of the world and from each other their true feelings until so intense is the hatred or jealousy being suppressed that it explodes in violent emotion and action.

"It would have been better in the eyes of God," Dowell comments, "if they had all attempted to gouge out each other's eyes with carving knives. But they were 'good people'" (249). It is significant that Dowell says "they" not "we," for if he had included himself it might have been his saving grace. It is Dowell who provides the "shock-proof world" for Florence. It is Dowell who displays no emotion on the death of his wife. It is Dowell who watches on the sidelines the game of shuttlecocks being played by the Ashburnhams and Nancy Rufford (Leonora's attempt to draw him into the "game" by suggesting he marry Nancy after Florence's death is unsuccessful). And it is Dowell who, knowing that Edward is about to commit suicide, does nothing to hinder it; he does not even comment, thinking that perhaps it would not be quite good form to say, "God bless you."

We are brought full circle to the anecdote that provided the *donnée* for *The Good Soldier*. For what is "appalling" ultimately —the final effect to which the novel has progressed in its last words—is that Dowell, Ashburnham's pale American image, is unable to say anything, even something sentimental, for fear of breaching "English good form." In the face of his friend's direct, challenging glare, he asks himself, "Why should I hinder him? I didn't think he was wanted in the world [. . .]" (256). A word, an action, might have saved the girl from madness and Edward from self-destruction, for "he was wanted in the world."

Thus, the novel ends on a double note of tragic irony. Dowell's failure to interfere, his neutrality in a world of violent, warring personalities, is as much if not more a cause of madness and self-destruction as Leonora's being pleased with the telegram which represents her triumph over Edward in the game of shuttlecocks. It is an appalling victory; Nancy and Edward were sacrificed to achieve Leonora's "happy ending with wedding bells and all" (252); for now she is free to marry Rodney Bayham and live a happy, normal life. Yet what is more appalling is Dowell's life as caretaker to Nancy, who to all appearances is a perfectly healthy and beautiful girl, whom Dowell is now "free" to marry but cannot because her reason will never be restored. The world will never be the same again though it will survive, as Leonora does, for "society must go on," but to Dowell who must nurse it—"it is a picture without a meaning."

CHAPTER 4

"The Whole Design":
The Marsden Case *and* Parade's End

I The Marsden Case

*T*HE MARSDEN CASE (1923), Ford's first novel in eight years and published just a year before the appearance of the first volume of the Tietjens tetralogy, is something of a disappointment for the reader of Ford who seeks to find a continuity of achievement and development from *The Good Soldier* to *Some Do Not. . . .* The same method of having the story "told" by a first-person narrator who attempts "to reproduce the story only as it occurred to my attention and as it now comes back to me"[1] is used, as in *The Good Soldier*; and the same two-part structure, the contrast of pre-war and wartime settings, and a similar kind of beleaguered protagonist who is vilified and slandered unjustly are used as in *Some Do Not. . . .*

And yet in the treatment of these methods the novel fails. The narrator, Ernest Jessop, unlike John Dowell, is only an accidental and reluctant witness who is sometimes a mere recorder and reporter of the events that nearly drive the protagonist, George Heimann Marsden, to repeat his father's death by suicide. There is neither the personal involvement of the narrator to draw the reader into the dark forest of the heart, as in *The Good Soldier*, nor the symbolic significance of the protagonist, as in *Some Do Not . . .* , to rescue the story from its complicated details of litigation and scandal. Too much of the second half of the novel is devoted to a detailed exposition of the litigation and scandal; as a result, the second part lacks the dramatic unity and intensity of the first part.

The story involves an old scandal, dimly remembered, that Lord Marsden, George's father, had appropriated for the government an invention without adequate compensation to the inventor; hounded by the press and undeservedly driven out of political office, he changed his name and went into exile in Germany. The outbreak of the war ended any chances of his ever being reinstated, and in despair he committed suicide. The sins of the father are visited upon the children, for his son George and his daughter Marie Elizabeth suffer because of Marsden's well-intentioned attempt to protect them from scandal by not letting them know who their father was and not legally providing for their inheritance. As a result, George is convinced he is an illegitimate son.

Hounded by the press over a different litigation and involved in a complicated legal maneuver to gain the Marsden title and estate, George is vilified as a German spy, driven out of the army, and in despair attempts to commit suicide. He is rescued only at the last moment by the woman he loves and later marries, Clarice Honeywill. "Thus, simply, they entered Paradise" (322). Though the ending seems to be an all's-well-that-ends-well one, it is intended as a terrible irony, a fool's Paradise: all that George suffered was unnecessary; but, having suffered, he has learned nothing from it.

War, Jessop says, is a terrible thing and unnecessary, but having suffered it, the world has learned nothing from it: "[. . .] the old evils, the old heartbreaks and the old cruelties are unceasingly at work," (305) leading toward another war. In the last chapter, George Heimann, now Lord Marsden, is every inch a nobleman, holding a ten-pound note over the head of the waiter who has spilled sauce on his boots and who is on his knees wiping it up; George is holding over the man his fate, whether he will be fired or not. The final emphasis is not, however, on class warfare—on the aristocracy versus the proletariat—but on what has been suffered and lost in the war; for the waiter had been the proprietor of a grand hotel in Eastern Europe and lost it, his wife had been murdered and his daughter carried off. But to Lord Marsden and his circle the situation is merely an amusing, though slightly embarrassing, incident. Jessop, the novelist-narrator, who sympathized with George in his sufferings, now feels for the waiter; but Jessop, who still holds to the old values of decency, is an outsider in the post-war world.

II   Parade's End *as a Multiple Novel*

While *The Marsden Case* does not enhance Ford's reputation at this stage in his development as a novelist, it does indicate the direction of his concern that came to fruition in *Parade's End*. *The Good Soldier* chronicles the psychological and moral disintegration of pre-war society leading to the holocaust of war. *Parade's End* successfully portrays what *The Marsden Case* only partially suggests: "[. . .] how mournful, how terrible, and how long a strain on the mind the war really was" (305). There are no battle scenes in *The Marsden Case,* and George Heimann's mind is so involved with the strain of litigation and concern over the legitimacy of his birth that the war itself, though he is in the army for a time, does not seem to touch him. The stress on the mind is more poignantly captured by Ford in the vignette of the waiter who had had a frightful nervous breakdown, not during the war but upon the declaration of peace; yet even this is related by the narrator in contrast to the direct portrayal of the mental breakdown of Christopher and Mark Tietjens in *Parade's End.*

As with *The Good Soldier,* the *donnée* for *Parade's End* was an anecdote about actual persons. In *It Was the Nightingale,* Ford reveals that his friend, Arthur Marwood, told a story about a mutual friend who married a woman because she had convinced him she was pregnant by him, but he later doubts whether the child is his because of her continual unfaithfulness. He is tormented by these doubts, but his gentleman's code of decency and his wife's Catholicism prevent his divorcing her. What is doubly significant is that Marwood not only supplied the anecdote that Ford used as the central situation in his tetralogy, but that Marwood was also the model for the protagonist, Christopher Tietjens.

Ford described Marwood in *It Was the Nightingale*: "There he was, large—an 'elephant built out of meal sacks.' Deliberate, slow in movement and extraordinarily omniscient. He was physically very strong and enduring. And he was, beneath the surface, extraordinarily passionate—with an abiding passion for the sort of truth that makes for intellectual accuracy in the public service.

It was a fascinating task to find him a posthumous career."[2] Marwood himself, though appearing to be physically strong and enduring, was tubercular and lived a sedentary life in Kent where he died of tuberculosis. Thus, though Marwood, a Tory, was "a man of infinite benevolence, comprehensions and knowledges" like Tietjens, and possessed "the power of cool observation in tremendous crises," Ford wanted a protagonist who was "enough of a man of action to get into the trenches and do what he was told."

In addition, Ford explains in his dedicatory letter to *No More Parades* that Tietjens' marital problems "[. . .] were suggested by the fate of a poor fellow living in a place in the south of France in which I happened to be stopping when I began the book [*Some Do Not . . .*, in 1922]. His misfortunes were much those of my central character, but he drank himself to death, it was said deliberately, after he had taken his wife back."[3] Yet another anecdote suggested the central triangle of *Parade's End*. A neighbor of Harold Munro had fallen in love after his wife ran off with another man; but his wife, who returned to him, refused to divorce him, and he committed suicide in despair. As Ford states, his protagonist was not to commit suicide but would "live his predicament down" (*It Was the Nightingale*, 221).

Ford, however, did not begin merely with a "plot" suggested by these anecdotes and then decide to expand it into a tetralogy. He deliberately set out to write a multiple novel about his own time. As Ford stated in explaining the genesis of *Parade's End*, what he "[. . .] wanted to see done was something on an immense scale, a little cloudy in immediate attack but with the salient points and the final impression extraordinarily clear. I wanted the Novelist in fact to appear in his really proud position as historian of his own time. Proust being dead I could see no one who was doing that . . ." (*It Was the Nightingale*, 199). Although Proust's *A la Recherche du Temps Perdu* had not been completely published by the time Ford began writing his tetralogy, enough of it had appeared to suggest the pattern and the technique of the whole with its recapture of personal history to reflect the degeneration of the social and moral order of the times.

Even earlier, Arnold Bennett had begun to publish his *Clayhanger* trilogy (1910-1916), in which he explored the impact of a changing, pre-war social order on the Clayhanger family. In

1915 Dorothy Richardson published *Pointed Roofs*, the first of a series of twelve novels in which she probes the inner psychology of her protagonist, Miriam, through the use of the stream-of-consciousness technique. And in 1922, the same year that Ford began work on his tetralogy, John Galsworthy published his *Forsyte Saga* (already published earlier as single novels) as a trilogy in a single volume, contrasting two social orders in a world of change and social upheaval. *In Chancery*, the second volume, ends with the funeral of Queen Victoria; and *To Let*, the third volume, shows the disintegration of that Victorian social order by setting its characters in post-war London, though the war itself is not directly portrayed. Also, 1922 saw the publication of Virginia Woolf's *Jacob's Room* and of James Joyce's *Ulysses* which, though single novels, further develop the stream-of-consciousness technique, with its use of the interior monologue first introduced by Dujardin in *Les Lauriers sont coupés* (1888), a technique which Ford uses in *Parade's End*. *Ulysses* and Woolf's *Mrs. Dalloway* (1925) combine the stream-of-consciousness technique with the narrative structure of recounting one day in the lives of the characters that Ford uses in *The Last Post*, and all three attempt to achieve the effect of simultaneity, a moment in time rendered in depth.

Whether or not Ford was directly influenced by experimenters like Proust, Joyce, and Woolf—Ford himself denied it—is not of paramount importance. My intention, rather, is to suggest that Ford belongs rightfully in the mainstream of the modern experimental novel and that he contributed to the development of its techniques. Cassell suggests that Ford seems to have arrived at the stream-of-consciousness technique as a natural development of his earlier techniques (254); and Ford, conscious as he was of technique, could have seen by himself the possibilities of extending Flaubert's method of depicting the inner consciousness through indirect speech. Of the multiple novels published before *Parade's End*, only Proust's *A la Recherche du Temps Perdu* is so interrelated that the design of the whole is dependent on the final novel and the whole is a single novel; but that final volume was not published until 1927, the same year Ford finished writing *The Last Post*. This interdependence of the four novels so that they are in effect a single novel is a logical extension of the *progression d'effet* that we have observed in *The Good Soldier*.

As Robie Macauley has observed, *Parade's End* is "one novel divided into four different books and I think it can be comprehended in no other way."[4] And Ford wrote in 1931, "I think *The Good Soldier* is my best book technically, *unless you read the Tietjens books as one novel, in which case the whole design appears.*"[5]

The whole design of *Parade's End* is seen if one thinks of the tetralogy as a four-part structure of a single novel, similar in a sense to the structure of *The Good Soldier. Some Do Not . . .* (1924), the first "part," begins with pre-war England as its setting; and *The Last Post* (1928), the fourth "part" set in post-war England, provides a contrast to the two middle volumes, which are set during the war up to and including Armistice Day. *Some Do Not . . .* , divided into nearly equal halves, is in itself a balance of contrasts between pre-war complacency and wartime distintegration of values and traditions. Similarly, *A Man Could Stand Up—*(1926) contrasts the joyful celebration of peace on Armistice Day, when a man could stand up, with the agony of warfare, when a man must bury himself in trenches. Only *No More Parades* (1925) is set entirely within the war period, contrasting with *The Last Post*, the only volume set entirely within peacetime. In *No More Parades*, Sylvia Tietjens' private war against Christopher coalesces with Tietjens' career as a soldier at the front, and in *The Last Post* Sylvia declares an armistice in her war because she is unable and unwilling to pursue the enemy any further—just as the world, sick of war, refused to follow Mark Tietjens' cold logic of victory and pursue the Germans into Germany.

The central focus of the tetralogy is Christopher Tietjens; he is decidedly the protagonist of the first three volumes. Although he does not appear directly in *The Last Post*, except briefly at the very end, he is very much in the thoughts of the principal characters, particularly Mark Tietjens, the principal consciousness of this last book. *The Last Post*, because of the shift in focus from Christopher to Mark Tietjens and because of the prominence given to characters who, like Marie Léonie, Mark's wife, and young Mark, Sylvia's son, were only referred to in the earlier books, has caused at least one critic to dismiss it from the tetralogy.[6] A satisfactory reading of *The Last Post* in relation to the other three books is essential to our understanding of *Parade's*

End as a multiple novel. It is sufficient to say at this point that the key to the relationship of this last novel to the other three is, as in the Dowell-Ashburnham relationship in *The Good Soldier*, the double focus of Christopher and Mark Tietjens as alter egos. Thus, though Christopher Tietjens is physically absent through most of the novel, he is "present" not only in the thoughts of the characters but also symbolically in Mark.

The *progression d'effet* of *Parade's End* is achieved, as in *The Good Soldier*, by the recurrence of leading motifs. Key scenes, images, and themes become motifs which recur in later volumes so that the total effect is cumulative. These motifs—such as Tietjens' doubts whether he is the father of his son, his night ride with Valentine in the dog cart, Sylvia's interview with Father Consett, animal imagery and the mud image, all of which appear in *Some Do Not . . .* , the seminal volume of the tetralogy—provide an interlocking movement so that the four books are a single novel. Their recurrence in Christopher Tietjens' mind and their significance as seen from the different points of view of other characters create an interrelated pattern of progression by which we interpret the whole.

As in *The Good Soldier*, time shift is the controlling narrative method by which these leading motifs are introduced or recalled. Certain key days are used to render the history of that period as reflected in the lives of the characters (the obvious historical ones being the day war was declared and Armistice Day). Flashbacks are used to re-create a scene, or, as in *A Man Could Stand Up—*, a whole section takes us back in time from Armistice Day to Tietjens months earlier in the trenches at the front. What is different from *The Good Soldier* is that the stream-of-consciousness technique with its device of association of ideas enabled Ford to recall a whole scene or impression from the past with a word, phrase, or visual image which in turn illuminates both past and present and links them in the consciousness of the character. Thus the tetralogy progresses organically rather than literally so that each novel is an essential part of the whole organism.

The title of each of the four novels is the theme of that novel so that the titles are in themselves motifs, which, taken together, become the whole theme in progression. Thus, "some do not" is essentially the idea that Christopher Tietjens as an English, Tory, Christian gentleman does not display his emotions publicly, wallow in the mud of scandal, shirk his duty, betray his principles of honor and decency for selfish gains, nor destroy the reputations of others for the sake of saving his own. But, if some do not, some do; and it is apparent in the second half of *Some Do Not . . .* and throughout the rest of the tetralogy, that most do act selfishly and dishonorably, representing the disintegration of traditional values not so much caused by the war as accelerated by it. There will be "no more parades" because the war has seen the end of individual honor and glory. "A man could stand up" on a hill out of the trenches, out of the mud, only when peace has come and "the last post" is sounded. Armistice is declared and the war ended, both in the epic struggle of the world and in the private war of Sylvia against Tietjens; but the world as it existed before the Flood is destroyed by its own willful evilness; and the new will lack the landmarks of the old: those principles of conscience and duty that "are like a skeleton map of a country."

III   Some Do Not . . .

Since the title motif recurs throughout the novel at crucial points and since new meanings become attached to it as the novel develops, it becomes a device by which both the structure and the theme are revealed. In *Some Do Not . . .* , the first explicit reference to the title occurs at the end of the first chapter; Macmaster quotes to himself the couplet, "The gods to each ascribe a differing lot:/Some enter at the portal. Some do not!" The context of the quotation is Macmaster's envy of Tietjens' upper-class associations; the deference paid to him by others; the easy acquaintanceship with generals, lords, and ladies; the unconcern for personal appearance whereas Macmaster must keep up appearances. The irony is that, as the tetralogy progresses, their positions are reversed. Macmaster is knighted and honored while Tietjens appears to be benighted and dishonored; yet the truth is that Macmaster achieves his knighthood at the loss of personal integrity while Tietjens loses everything but his integrity.

Irony is pervasive in *Parade's End*, as it is in *The Good Soldier*; it is the controlling tone of the whole tetralogy. From the very beginning of *Some Do Not . . .* the ironic tone is established, and the basic theme of the discrepancy between appearances and reality is implied. Tietjens and Macmaster, the one a Tory and the other a Whig, are sitting in a "perfectly appointed railway carriage" on a train that runs as smoothly "as British gilt-edged securities," the only swayings or jolts along the line being those that are "expected and allowed for." But these two young men, both representatives of the ruling class who administer the world, though one is a Tietjens of Groby and the other the son of a shopkeeper, are in reality riding with the rest of the world— smoothly and comfortably in first-class style—toward disaster. The train, itself the symbol of pre-war pride in the material progress of man, symbolizes the appearance of man's well-being which hides the moral weakness within, as long as things are going smoothly.

As in Conrad's *Heart of Darkness*, dehumanized efficiency is at the heart of modern evil. Both Tietjens and Macmaster administer the newly created Imperial Department of Statistics, a symbol of modern efficiency and dehumanization. As a soldier, Tietjens' one contribution to the war for which he is praised is the efficiency with which he is able to dispatch units of draftees to the front. Macmaster is knighted for his efficient use of statistics to "prove" that the devastation of war was no more than what one might expect from a normal year's losses in household dilapidations (a false use of statistics which Tietjens had refused to do). Even Mark Tietjens contributes to the efficiency of modern warfare by effectively administering the Transport Office. All this efficiency is to be seen against the background of a world-wide conflict that is scientifically organized and impersonally mechanized and administered by the same class which saw to it that the trains ran smoothly.

Though directly alluded to only five times in the novel, the "some do not" motif is implicit throughout. At the beginning in a flashback to the day Sylvia left Christopher to run off with Drake, Macmaster declares: "I wish you would drag the woman through the mud." Gentlemen do not drag their ladies through the mud of scandal even though they have sufficient evidence for divorce. As a result, Tietjens himself is dragged through the mud by Sylvia. Tietjens' distaste for public scandal becomes, in *No More Parades*, a physical fear of mud. Trench warfare with its mounds of mud becomes the visible symbol for all the accumulated slime of scandal clinging to Tietjens as a result of

Sylvia's personal war against him, for the hypocrisy and betrayal of the soldiers in the trenches by the civilian ruling class at home, and for the whole rottenness of a world at war.

Sylvia's private war against Tietjens is not a mere aberration caused by the moral dislocation of war (indeed, she declares war long before the nations do); hers is Satan's war against God through man, and the World War itself is a reflection of original sin. In her interview with Father Consett, God's representative on earth, Sylvia threatens to torment Tietjens by corrupting her child: "I'll get even with him. I can. I know how, you see. And with you, through him, for tormenting me." Father Consett threatens to exorcise the devil in her: "She erected her body above her skirts on the sofa, stiffened like a *snake's neck above its coils.*" She leaves the room, banished by Father Consett, "her black figure showed in silhouette against the open doorway" (41, Italics mine).

The allegory suggested in this scene is fundamental to an understanding of Ford's rendering of man's war with the forces of evil outside of himself and within himself. Tietjens, as Adam, is essentially a good man; but he is hated for knowing everything, what Sylvia calls the sheer immorality of his views. The good man, the gentleman, is vulnerable to the attacks of evil because he will not fight back with the same weapons ("no gentleman thinks such things of his wife") and because his very actions, no matter how honorable and well-intentioned, can be used against him. Sylvia's campaign of vilification against Tietjens must be seen in the light of this allegorical intention—not that the whole tetralogy is an allegory but that the theme of good and evil, related as it is to the idea of appearance and reality, is metaphysical in essence.

Ironically, Sylvia declares war against good by deciding to be virtuous and to return to Tietjens and remain faithful to him. Tietjens, who "stands for monogamy and chastity," torments himself for having had sexual relations with Sylvia before marriage: "if it's sexual sins God punishes, He indeed is just and inscrutable!" (121). For his punishment is to live with Sylvia, a damnation to a hell that is "a cavernous eternity of weary hopelessness" (121). Ford skillfully combines a modern psychological interpretation of sexual guilt with a traditional religious sense of sin and damnation. Tietjens, having rationally decided to take

Sylvia back for the sake of her reputation, momentarily loses control of himself in front of Macmaster: "He nearly vomited; his brain reeled and the room fell about. He drank an enormous quantity of whisky in front of Macmaster's goggling eyes; but even at that he couldn't talk, and he dropped into his bed faintly aware of his friend's efforts to loosen his clothes. He had, he knew, carried the suppression of thought in his conscious mind so far that his unconscious self had taken command and had, for the time, paralysed both his body and his mind" (80).

Some do not . . . philander. Tietjens' decision to take back Sylvia coincides with his meeting Valentine Wannop. The key scene of their relationship in *Some Do Not . . .* is the night ride in the dog-cart at the end of Part One. This idyllic ride, during which Tietjens suppresses an impulse to kiss Valentine because married gentlemen do not, ends in disaster. Appearances are against Tietjens; General Campion is convinced he has been philandering with Valentine, and this incident becomes the basis for much of the gossip about Tietjens.

The dog-cart crashes into General Campion's automobile just as Tietjens, his vision still obscured by the mist, says, "We're all right now!" An examination in some detail of this accident reveals much about Ford's technique and the interrelationships of the various parts of the tetralogy. The night ride is a parallel to the train ride which begins the novel, and by extension it reveals the unexpected jolt that ends the peaceful ride. The sound of the crash is like the scraping of "twenty tea-trays, a prolonged sound" (139), which is the impressionistic image used to describe the sound of the artillery bombardment which begins *No More Parades*. The ammunition for Sylvia's private war is provided by this incident, by Tietjens himself as it were; for General Campion and the others are ready to believe the worst of him as a result.

The horse is severely wounded in the accident, and Tietjens binds the wound, feeling responsible. The fly-driver who happens along at the moment says that some are merciful to their beasts; but as for himself, he "wouldn't leave my little wooden 'ut, nor miss my breakfast, for no beast" (144). Tietjens' conscience requires him to accept the responsibility for the horse ("the poor beast had trusted him and he had smashed it up"), just as at the beginning of *No More Parades* his sense of guilt makes him accept responsibility for the death of O Nine Morgan who died bleeding in his arms, and later, in *A Man Could Stand Up—*, for blinding Sergeant Aranjuez.

Freedom from the responsibility for one's own actions and the actions of others is a romantic illusion: the mist which obscures his vision obscures the reality of his situation until the accident is inevitable, just as earlier, his head clear of the mist but the rest of him obscured, he could believe himself free of responsibilities, free to give in to his impulse to kiss Valentine. This image of the mist finds its echo in the mud image in *No More Parades* and in *A Man Could Stand Up—*; and in *The Last Post* Mark Tietjens recalls the apocryphal story of the Yorkshireman who, standing on Mount Ararat with the water up to his chin, says "It's boon to tak oop!" Tietjens is brought back to the reality of his responsibilities, guided by his principles: "Principles are like a skeleton map of a country—you know whether you're going east or north" (144).

The next reference to the some-do-not motif occurs near the middle of Part Two, and it is spoken by the staff officer who, in commenting on Tietjens' insistence on being sent to the front, says: "Some do. Some do not." The context, however, links the motif to the Sylvia-Valentine triangle. Tietjens, determined to have sexual relations with Valentine before he leaves for the front the next day, is subconsciously disturbed that Sylvia may after all be in love with him. His motivation then in wanting to go to the front seems a solution to this "impossible complication. [. . .] the best thing for him was to go and get wiped out as soon as possible" (224).

The death-wish suggested must also be seen in relation to Tietjens' conviction that the civilization he knew and loved is doomed: "I've nothing to live for: what I stand for isn't any more in this world. What I want, as you know, I can't have" (237). His conscience will not allow him to use his mind to contribute to the war (as Macmaster and Mark Tietjens do); but he is not a pacifist as Valentine is (his sense of duty will not allow that), so he will sacrifice his "great, hulking body." It is significant that what Tietjens fears most at the front (*No More Parades* and *A Man Could Stand Up—*) is not physical death but mental breakdown; he has already had a case of amnesia induced by shell-shock (*Some Do Not . . .*); but, if he survived, he would be purged, "a man with cleaned, sand-dried bones: a clear mind" (187). On the other hand, Mark Tietjens' paralysis (*The Last Post*) suggests the mental aberration of war; for, though Mark's illness is physically real, his withdrawal from the world is a sickness symbolic of the post-war withdrawal from responsibilities.

The final recurrences of the motif come at the end of the novel. The first, mouthed by an old tramp as he watches Valentine weeping, epitomizes the sexual contempt in which young women in love are viewed by old men: "That's women! . . . Some do!" Even his afterthought is not a salute to chastity but a revelation of contempt: "Ah! . . . Some do not!" The irony is that appearances are close to the truth; for, though the old tramp assumes Valentine is already weeping for her lost virginity, the truth is that Valentine has just agreed to become Tietjens' mistress. Yet finally, though the rest of the world takes the tramp's view of Tietjens and Valentine, it is Tietjens himself who says, "We're the sort that . . . *do not!*"

Animal imagery provides another repetitive pattern by which the design of the whole is revealed. The walls of Mrs. Satterthwaite's sitting room "were completely covered with pictures of animals in death agonies: capercailzies giving up the ghost with gouts of scarlet blood on the snow; deer dying with their heads back and eyes glazing, gouts of red blood on their necks; foxes dying with scarlet blood on green grass" (26). The contrast between these pictures "representing sport" and the civilized comfort of the other furnishings is the contradiction between man's civilized ideals and his predatory nature; even Mrs. Satterthwaite confesses to a nearly uncontrollable, predatory desire "to put my nails into the veins" of a man's neck. "And it's worse with Sylvia," she continues, "It's a natural antipathy" (27).

Sylvia refers to Tietjens as the Ox, the sacrificial animal; and her getting Tietjens to marry her is referred to by the trapper's term, trepanning. Sylvia's satanic appearance is associated with the pictures when Father Consett, pointing to one of a wild boar dying with its throat cut, hisses, "*Sport!* . . . It's devilry!" These pictures are in obvious contrast to Tietjens' merciful and sentimental attention to the bleeding horse. What is less obvious is that the idea of sportsmanship, of playing the game as one has been taught to do in school, will not do in a predatory society where the law of the jungle predominates whether it is in politics, love or war:

You look at a dozen men, each of them not by any means detestable and not uninteresting, for each of them would have technical details of their affairs to impart; you formed them into a Government or a club and at once, with oppressions, inaccuracies, gossip, backbiting, lying, corruptions and vileness, you had the combination of wolf, tiger, weasel and louse-covered ape that was human society. And he remembered the words of some Russian: "Cats and monkeys. Monkeys and cats. All humanity is there" (79).

Mrs. Wannop's comforting morality—"The only thing that matters is to do good work"—will not do in a wilderness of howling, squalling monkeys because in such a world good work is a sign of weakness. Tietjens' good works become the basis for further scandals which destroy his personal reputation.

The predatory image associated with Sylvia is the hawk which preys on the gulls which in turn prey on the herring of the sea. In contrast, Valentine is associated with the songbirds: the goldfinch, the chaffinch. Tietjens contrasts the two women as opposites: he respects "the one for sheer efficiency in killing; the other for having the constructive desire and knowing how to set about it" (128). The novel, and indeed the whole tetralogy, is patterned by such sharp contrasts: Tietjens and Macmaster, Tory and Whig; Sylvia and Valentine, predator and pacifist; Christopher and Mark Tietjens, idealist and pragmatist; peace and war; some do, some do not. The structure itself is a two-part contrast between pre-war and wartime settings, but what becomes clear in *Some Do Not . . .* , and is borne out in the rest of the tetralogy, is that war is an intensification rather than a cause of evil. Macmaster's falsification of the statistics is a logical extension of his ambition to achieve class status and thus "enter at the portal"; when the war presented the opportunity, his lack of personal integrity took advantage of this. Sylvia's determination to ruin Tietjens arises out of her evil nature; the war provides the atmosphere in which her unnatural machinations against Tietjens seem natural and normal because the whole of society has become degenerate and corrupt.

Parade's End is not a war novel in the sense of being concerned with the historical causes of war or with the reconstruc-

tion of actual battles; it is essentially a psychological novel in
which the causes of war are traced back to psychological causes
for conflict in man. Moral problems of individuals—and Ford
ultimately saw war as a moral crisis for individual nations—are
rooted in psychological ones, primarily sexual in origin. Ford
does not, however, take the position that moral standards are
merely reflections of sexual repressions and taboos; he does
suggest, as in *The Good Soldier*, that the English characteristic
of suppressing emotions causes the Englishman "to go to pieces
very badly" in moments of unusual stresses. Good and evil are
real qualities in the metaphysical sense in *Parade's End*, but
they are inseparably linked with sexual attitudes.

The war, therefore, is related to the breakdown of moral
standards among nations; and the breakdown of moral standards
in a nation is related to psychological pressures in the individual.
Sylvia, berating Tietjens for his lack of emotionalism, speaks a
truth with which Tietjens agrees: " 'If,' Sylvia went on with her
denunciation, 'you had once in our lives said to me: 'You whore!
You bitch! You killed my mother. May you rot in hell for it. . . .
If you'd only once said something like it . . . about the child!
About Perowne! . . . you might have done something to bring us
together . . .' " (172).

Tietjens' and Valentine's decision that they are "the sort that
. . . do not" is a sexual denial based on moral principles that has
its psychological repercussions later on for Tietjens at the front
and for Valentine on Armistice Day. Yet their denial is not believed by any one else, for in a society without moral standards
chastity is implausible and unbelievable. In contrast, Sylvia's
sexual denial is rooted in her psychological contempt for men;
her "chastity" gives her a sense of triumph over men. Yet her
hatred of Tietjens arises out of her sexual desire which is frustrated by his refusal; and thus her war against him is motivated
by a very human sexual jealousy as well as by an allegorically
evil nature.

Thus, the psychological conflict within man is the focus of the
tetralogy, and the war itself is a reflection of that conflict.
Tietjens at the very beginning links the war with moral and
sexual causes: "War [. . .] is inevitable. [. . .] Simply because
you fellows are such damn hypocrites. [. . .] We're always, as it
were, committing adultery [. . .] with the name of Heaven on

our lips" (20). On the day before war is declared Valentine has a shock when Mrs. Duchemin asks her where she might get an abortion, and on the next day Tietjens rides with Mrs. Duchemin on the train, which becomes the basis for the gossip about Tietjens that not only Valentine is his mistress but also Mrs. Duchemin. Tietjens' decision to offer his body as a sacrifice to the war because his conscience will not let him use his brain in its service is the counterpart of his denial of his body for the sake of a principle. Valentine's willingness to become Tietjens' mistress is a momentary surrender to the temper of the times, for in a world where there will be no more parades (foreshadowing the theme of No More Parades and thus linking the two novels), "Chastity: na poo finny! Like everything else!" (266). On Armistice Day Valentine rebels against this "nun-like" denial of her flesh and becomes Tietjens' mistress (A Man Could Stand Up—).

Sylvia's fidelity to Tietjens is the ironic counterpart of Valentine's; it comes too late for reconciliation. Already Tietjens and Valentine are in love (ironically, their being linked together in gossip irresistibly draws them together "as in a carpenter's vice"). Sylvia's unfaithfulness before marriage is to Tietjens a betrayal of their love; on the night before leaving for the wedding in Paris, he confessed to Macmaster: "She's bitched me." Yet his own moral scruples and sexual guilt feelings will not allow him to berate her. Later he confesses to Macmaster, "I don't even know if the child's my own!" (15).

This anxiety of identity is a recurring motif throughout the tetralogy; it underlies the whole duality of contrasts in Parade's End and underscores the discrepancy between appearances and reality. The only certainty is that Sylvia was pregnant before her marriage; but, if maternity is a matter of fact, paternity is a matter of opinion! The thought that Sylvia might have lured him to have sexual relations before their marriage so that she could claim the child was his is too much for Tietjens; he is jolted out of such thoughts by the fear that he has just had a stroke: "But he hadn't had a stroke. It must then, he thought, be that the pain of his last consideration must be too great for his mind to register, as certain great physical pains go unperceived" (122).

This physical shock, when Christopher for a moment believes his legs are paralyzed from a stroke, is the thematic counterpart to Mark Tietjens' real stroke brought on by the mental shock of learning that the defeated German army will not be pursued into Germany, thus linking *Some Do Not . . .* and *The Last Post.* Christopher survives because, refusing to use his brains to further the war, he physically purges himself in the war though the war leaves its mark on him. Mark dies (his withdrawal from the world is already a kind of death) because, using his brains during the war, he has died spiritually; his cold, logical strategy of victory is the dehumanized logistics of transport problems which a world, physically sick of war, rebels against.

Just before he dies, Mark Tietjens comes to the conclusion that Christopher is the father of Sylvia's son; and he bases his decision on the fact that the boy *looks* like Christopher and that the boy is his true nephew because he has fallen in love with "the same type of woman as his uncle"! Certainly from the very beginning of the tetralogy we are given the strong impression that the boy is *not* Christopher's son. This reversal in the last book of the tetralogy (coming as it does immediately after Mark reverses himself about his father's having committed suicide and Valentine's being his father's illegitimate daughter) *seems* to be a "sentimental indulgence,"[7] but if it is sentimentality it is indulged in by Mark Tietjens the character, not by Ford Madox Ford the author.

One must always keep in mind the basic irony of *Parade's End;* appearances are deceptive. *The Last Post* is consistent in ironic tone with *Some Do Not . . .* , for Mark decides that Christopher is the boy's father on no more solid evidence than he or anyone else had for believing all the gossip about Christopher earlier. What must be understood, to understand the quality of irony in *Parade's End,* is that the human mind creates its own heaven or hell, depending on how appearances are interpreted. At the end of *Some Do Not . . .* Christopher and Valentine declare that they loved each other at first sight; in reality, Valentine's first impression of Christopher was of "a fat golfing idiot" and Christopher's first impression of her was of "a perfectly negligible girl except for the frown." At the end of *The Last Post*, Mark Tietjens, applying the same kind of reasoning that had led him to the conclusion that his father's death was an accident when an hour before he had convinced himself it was suicide, decides the boy is Christopher's son when an hour before he was convinced of the opposite. Appearances have their own reality in human relationships. Though they may be deceptive and false, people act upon them as though they were true.

IV   No More Parades

The theme of *No More Parades*, like that of *Some Do Not . . .*, is found in the repetitive motif of the title. The oft-quoted passage near the beginning of *No More Parades*, spoken by Tietjens, explicitly states the theme: " 'Don't you see how symbolical it was —the band playing *Land of Hope and Glory*, and then the adjutant saying *There will be no more parades?* . . . For there won't. There won't, there damn well won't. . . . No more. Hope, no more Glory, no more parades for you and me any more. Nor for the country . . . nor for the world, I dare say . . . None . . . Gone . . . Na poo, finny! No . . . more . . . parades' " (306-7).

The repetition within the passage itself is emphatic; the repetition within the novel is extensive, expanding the meaning of the theme. The specific context of the motif is military ceremony, of being on parade; but the world of parades is an anachronism in a war where men "by the quarter million" could be massacred. The theme, however, has its implications in relation to the prewar world, thus linking it with *Some Do Not. . . .* The peaceful world of idyllic walks through English countryside—"God's England! [. . .] Land of Hope and Glory!" (106)—is shattered by the war. Even more specifically, that world was an illusion; for the romantic picture that Tietjens conjures up of himself and Valentine as a young couple in love admiring nature is obviously illusory; Tietjens is a married man and has thus already compromised their reputations, and all the hypocrites are ready "to spread the tale." The appearance of peace hides the corruption ready to war against personal reputations; the appearance of good manners and good form suppresses the violent emotions in human relationships. The war destroyed even the pretense to good form and exposed the rottenness that had always existed underneath. Tietjens, having just been informed by his brother Mark that their own father thought him "a bloody pimp living on women," comments on this unnaturalness by observing the dead leaves in the base of a fountain: "This civilisation had contrived a state of things in which leaves rotted by August. Well, it was doomed!" (217).

The motif is related to the idea of good form with its cere-
monious sense of good manners, of not creating a scene, of playing the game. "The curse of the army," Tietjens says, "was our
imbecile national belief that the game is more than the player.
That was our ruin, mentally, as a nation" (305-6). At that moment the body of O Nine Morgan, still bleeding, is brought in.
If Tietjens were a man without conscience, he could shrug his
shoulders and say "That's war"; but, since Tietjens' conscience
will not allow him to shrug it off, he feels responsible for Morgan's death. By association of ideas, the sight of the blood reminds
Tietjens of the wounded horse in *Some Do Not . . .* ; the link
here is not merely a remembrance of that earlier sight of blood,
it is the whole idea of responsibility. Some do not, like the fly-
driver, bother to "patch up a horse that has been badly hurt";
some do not, like the quartermaster, worry about casualties because to him the game is more than the player. Tietjens does,
though Morgan is beyond patching up; and "the glowing image
of the fellow's blood" becomes the symbol of his sense of guilt
although there was nothing he really could have done for Morgan
that would have avoided disaster one way or the other.

In contrast to Tietjens' individual conscience is the description that the war is being conducted from the sidelines by men
without conscience who view the soldiers as so many statistics in
the strategy of power: "All these men given into the hands of the
most cynically care-free intriguers in long corridors who made
plots that harrowed the hearts of the world. All these men toys,
all these agonies mere occasions for picturesque phrases to be
put into politicians' speeches without heart or even intelligence.
Hundreds of thousands of men tossed here and there in that
sordid and gigantic mud-brownness of midwinter . . ." (296).

The mechanization of war on a vast worldwide scale has made
individual heroism and personal glory typified by ceremonial
parade obsolete. Tietjens, composing a sonnet which Mackenzie
will translate into Latin, itself an anachronism amid the grim
business of conducting a mechanized war, amusingly twists the
motif around to rhyme with "soil": "No more parades, Not any
more, no *oil* . . ." (319). But we are immediately brought back
to the bitter reality of war by the intent of the sonnet to convey
the idea that where so many thousands die "there was no room

for swank, typified by expensive funerals. As you might say: No flowers by compulsion . . . No more parades!" (320).

Army discipline, however, steeped as it is in tradition, requires "parade." General Campion represents absolute faith in this tradition; but he is not a Colonel Blimp. For all Campion's blustering, he is well aware that the world of parade is dead, that his seventeenth-century faith in the triumph of good over evil is an anachronism in the twentieth century. Yet he must hold on to his faith or be lost; the duality of his attitude toward Tietjens represents the dichotomy of his views. On the one hand, he says to Tietjens, "I've such an absolute belief in your trustworthiness" (474); on the other, he unquestioningly believes all the gossip about Tietjens.

This duality is not an irrational contradiction of attitudes but the faith of a Christian gentleman (as Tietjens calls him at one point) who accepts appearances as realities because he himself would never act otherwise than straightforwardly. Furthermore, Campion believes, as does Tietjens, that the honor and reputation of a woman must be protected at all costs; a gentleman can do no less to preserve the sanctity of marriage and the home. But this ideal is lost in the modern world. Macmaster has been hypocritically carrying on an affair with Mrs. Duchemin who hypocritically is malicious in her gossip about Valentine and Tietjens; O Nine Morgan's wife has been living with a prizefighter who has threatened to kill Morgan; Captain McKechnie (Macmaster's nephew) is being driven mad by his unfaithful wife; and Sylvia has given up her lover Perowne only because she is bored with him. Tietjens says: ". . . there are . . . there used to be . . . in families of . . . position . . . On the part of the man . . . a certain . . . Call it . . . parade!" (492). Campion's answer is "Then there had better be no more parades"; for, if Tietjens is not willing to take the consequences, then he had better divorce Sylvia.

No More Parades ends with General Campion on parade; appearances must be kept up, at least in the army. At the beginning of *A Man Could Stand Up*— the post-war counterpart of the "no more parades" motif is expressed by Valentine on Armistice Day: "She had been through the mill: the whole world had been through the mill! No more respect!" (506). There will be no more respect "for constituted Authority and consecrated

Experience" (511). Part Two of *A Man Could Stand Up*– is a lengthy time shift back to the days immediately following the end of *No More Parades*, when General Campion in promoting Tietjens has also sent him to the front lines to be in command of a battalion. This section completes the meaning of the motif: Tietjens and Aranjuez stood up out of the trench; an artillery shell bursts at their feet, moving the mud which engulfs them; Tietjens works himself free and then rescues Aranjuez. It is, however, a violation of army regulations for an officer to so expose himself unnecessarily so that when Tietjens appears before General Campion, on parade but covered with mud, the General is so incensed by his unofficer-like appearance that he dismisses Tietjens from his command and sends him home in disgrace. The mud of scandal and disgrace clings to Tietjens no matter how good his intentions, just as in rescuing Aranjuez he blinds him.

In *No More Parades*, a physical fear of mud obsesses Tietjens: "It is unbearable: it is that that has ruined us. . . . The mud!" These words are spoken by a German deserter who, like the rest of his comrades who have deserted with him, is covered with mud, so that their coming to surrender seems like the mud itself is moving. Tietjens has yet to have his baptism of mud, but the slime of scandal, like the dishonor of desertion, is ruining him as surely as it did the German deserters. The mud image, with its picture of highly mechanized armies bogged down in the mud, suggests that the world itself is bogged down in its own slime. Ford, however, renders this idea through the specific machinations of Sylvia. It is in *No More Parades* that Sylvia's private war merges with world war so that the two are reflecting aspects of the same human agony, for Ford views the real suffering of the war to be mental rather than physical.

Sylvia dominates the middle section of the three-part structure of *No More Parades*, as Tietjens does the other two. It is significant that Valentine does not directly appear in this volume devoted entirely to the war, only reappearing again at the beginning of *A Man Could Stand Up*– when Armistice is declared. Indeed, in the whole teralogy the only scene set during the war in which Valentine takes part is the day before Tietjens is sent to France (*Some Do Not . . .*) when first she is repelled at the sight of Tietjens in uniform and accuses him of supporting the horror of

war and then later the same day she is willing to surrender herself to him, become his mistress, and defy the conventions and
overcome her prejudice against him as a soldier. Valentine, the
pacifist, has nothing to do with the war, and therefore her ab-
sence from the war scenes is no accident but rather is part of the
design of the whole. Furthermore, her denial of the flesh, a nun-
like vow of chastity, seems like a withdrawal from a world devoted to the flesh. In contrast, Sylvia, who had given Tietjens
the impression she would enter a convent and withdraw from
the world, is in France to carry the war to Tietjens.

Tietjens' belief that he had separated from Sylvia and was
quit of her and all the complications of their private lives is as
illusory as his belief that he could separate his mind from his
body and devote only the latter to the war. His life "off parade"
(private life) is entangled with his life "on parade" (as a soldier
on duty), just as the war itself is enmeshed in the machinations
of the civilians in power at home. Tietjens cannot escape from
the mental anguish of war because it is no longer an eighteenth-
century parade separating soldiers from civilians and conducted
by gentlemen officers from the best families, educated at the best
schools, and trained to be gentlemen first and officers second.
Nor can he escape the consequences of his private life, for, in a
world where there are no more parades, the public conflict is the
same as the private one. In such a world the only thing "is to be
able to stick to the integrity of your character, whatever earth-
quake sets the house tumbling over your head," (454) Tietjens
says to Colonel Levin; then, win or lose the war, one has achieved
victory over evil.

It is Sylvia's strategy to defeat Tietjens by setting the house
tumbling over his head, to make "his wooden face wince" by
humiliating him. She wars against him through General Campion
in the hope of ruining Tietjens as an officer. She accuses Tietjens
of being a Socialist and of wanting "to model himself upon our
Lord." It is characteristic of Ford's use of irony that he utilizes
a delightful sense of comic irony to render a serious theme. General (Lord) Campion at first obtusely misunderstands Sylvia's
accusation and asks "Who's that . . . our *Lord?*"; when he under-
stands, he is incensed and denies that Christ was a Socialist, for
"He said: Render under Caesar . . . It wouldn't be necessary to
drum Him out of the army" (412).

[114]

It would be easy enough (and critically fashionable) to suggest that Tietjens is a Christ figure: his name, Christopher, his mania for self-sacrifice, his duality of mind and body, his refusal to accept Groby, the mental anguish (deserted by his Father), the calumnies and slanders that press upon him like a crown of thorns, the burden of guilt he bears like a cross, and his "resurrection" at the end of the tetralogy after being "absent" (admittedly it was only for a day and a half, not three!). But too literal an allegorical interpretation obscures the full import of Ford's theme: the wasteland world will not only reject a Messiah and not recognize Him, but the Messiah himself does not understand his role.

At the end of *No More Parades*, Tietjens, after nearly ruining himself to protect Sylvia's reputation over Perowne, cries out in anguish, "*Why* the devil am I so anxious to shield that whore? It's not reasonable. It is an obsession" (495). The messianic personality itself is viewed in the modern world as a sexual manifestation so that Tietjens' problem is "the whole problem of the relations of the sexes" (491). The old image of God as a kind of great English landowner on a colossal scale with Christ as "an almost too benevolent Land-Steward, son of the Owner" (365), has been replaced by the modern image of God as "a Real Estate Agent, with Marxist views." Tietjens in the end, if he is still to be viewed as a Christ figure, is reduced to furnishing rich men's homes with period furniture, having renounced his stewardship of Groby.

Sylvia herself believes Tietjens is only "playing at being our Lord" forgiving the adulterous woman; his self-sacrifices are to her a manifestation of an outmoded chivalry. She had taken up with Perowne in a fit of sexual hatred, reacting against Tietjens' quality of mind (Perowne is the complete opposite of Tietjens); but, since Tietjens has spoiled her for other men, she is contemptuous of Perowne. She is sexually jealous of Valentine and vows she will never let Tietjens go; for, if she cannot have him, no one else will; she will use her Catholicism as a weapon. Perowne becomes a pawn in her strategy.

Reversing the traditional scene of domestic tragedy (or comedy) in which the jealous husband confronts the lover in his wife's bedroom, Sylvia maneuvers the situation so that Perowne breaks in on an apparently happy domestic scene of husband and wife together. It was to be her victory over Valentine by sleeping with Tietjens, over Tietjens by letting him know she had made an assignation with her lover Perowne, and over Perowne by showing her contempt for him and getting him into a compromising situation, a situation in which Tietjens would have to play his role of outraged husband. It becomes instead a comedy of errors with disastrous consequences for all concerned, but especially for Tietjens—he throws out Perowne thinking him a drunken French waiter who had ogled Sylvia earlier, he forcibly pushes out his superior officer General O'Hara who believed Tietjens was trying to blackmail Perowne, and Sylvia's reputation is endangered by her own machinations. The situation is salvaged by Tietjens' willingness to accept the blame, a trait Sylvia could count on if her strategy failed.

The victory is ultimately Tietjens' because he maintains his personal integrity, but the appearances are of defeat. Though General Campion releases him from arrest and actually promotes him, Tietjens' personal reputation is under an even darker cloud. General Campion, still believing in parade, says to him, "An officer's private life and his life on parade are as strategy to tactics" (478). What General Campion cannot forgive Tietjens are the complications of his private life; for, Campion says, no matter what the rights and wrongs of it, "you are a disaster to every one who has had to do with you" (481). Tietjens' explanation for this is significant: "In civilian life, sir, I was a statistician" (478). The dehumanized world of numbers has no room for a man with a conscience believing in an eighteenth-century ethical system, nor has the world of mechanized warfare room for the "last surviving Tory," whose sentimentality for horses is the symbol of his humanity.

When General Campion says of Tietjens to Sylvia that "Christopher is a regular Dreyfus," he echoes his earlier words to Tietjens in Some Do Not. . . . Ford apparently intended this statement as part of the "justification" for the seemingly motiveless malignancy by which others gossip about Tietjens and believe the worst about him. Ford's intention is not to go into the rights and wrongs of the Dreyfus case, but to suggest the kind of milieu that made it possible—and, perhaps more significantly, the chivalric personality that seems to attract such malignant calumnies. In this sense of attracting to himself the sins of others,

Tietjens can be interpreted as a Christ-figure. As General Campion says to Tietjens of Dreyfus in *Some Do Not . . .* ,

[. . .] "he was worse than guilty—the sort of fellow you couldn't believe in and yet couldn't prove anything against. The curse of the world. . . .
"[. . .] fellows like that *unsettle* society. You don't know where you are. You can't judge. They make you uncomfortable . . ." (75).

A modern Messiah becomes a Dreyfus or a Roger Casement (represented by Father Consett who is killed by the English), not a god. Sylvia expects a miracle to be performed by the martyred Father Consett before she will give up Tietjens and retire to a convent; General Campion expects Tietjens to "render unto Caesar" and yet retain his personal integrity.

No More Parades ends on a quiet note with the sound of General Campion's crop tapping the locker panel on his inspection tour of the cook houses. The novel began with the "enormous crashing sound" of an artillery shell bursting, and the next novel, *A Man Could Stand Up*—, begins with the "intolerable noises" of victory on Armistice Day. Yet the sound of the general's crop is to Tietjens "like the sudden bursting out of the regimental quick-step, as after a funeral with military honours the band and drums march away, back to barracks" (500). The *impression* is funereal, for the world of "parade" has died; and amid all the chaos of personal and military complications stands General Campion, "on parade," performing the ritual of inspection like a high-priest in a cathedral. The *progression d'effet* of the novel is the irony that the whole world of tradition, of "parade," is reduced to the meaningless, symbolic gesture of inspecting the battalion's pepper supply. With this paradox Ford portrays Armistice Day in the next volume—as the funeral knell of the old order and as the birth of the new.

V   A Man Could Stand Up—

The three-part structural pattern of *A Man Could Stand Up*— repeats the pattern of *No More Parades,* just as the last novel repeats the two-part structure of the first. *No More Parades,* as we have seen, alternates between the world conflict and the private conflict so that the two converge and are part of the same mental anguish that is the human condition. *A Man Could Stand Up—*, alternating between peace and war, reinforces this direct connection between mental tensions in personal human relationships and tensions between nations.

Ford viewed the Armistice as the end of something more than the physical fighting; it was a release from the mental, a sense of letting go: the cessation of hostilities caused an almost physical reaction against resuming pre-war mental and moral attitudes; for these attitudes had led to war—and the war was more mental than physical suffering because the physical conflict intensified the emotional one in man. Valentine's reluctance to take up with Tietjens again, to become involved in "the suffocating web of his imbroglios," is a reflection of the whole world having been "through the mill" and not wanting to become entangled again in the web of mental conflict. Like the rest of the world, Valentine "wanted some fun! Now!"

But the end of the war does not solve all problems; it does not wipe the slate clean and destroy the past. Valentine attempts to deny it by not mentioning Tietjens' name, but hers is a futile gesture. The past is very much on her mind, and even as she almost convinces herself she does not care, the mention of Tietjens' name by Miss Wanostrocht releases her from the taboo of denial. That the imbroglios of the past are not ended, that no armistice has yet been declared in the private war, is clearly indicated by the form in which Tietjens is reintroduced into Valentine's life—by Lady Macmaster's offer to bring them together again, for a price. Nothing has changed in the basic impasse of their triangle; for, though Tietjens and Sylvia are separated, she will not divorce him (ostensibly because she is a Catholic but actually because she does not want Valentine to have him); and he will not divorce her because he still holds to his code that a gentleman does not divorce his wife.

Yet everything has changed since that night they had decided they were "the sort that do not": the middle-class morality, the Victorian principles on which their denial was based have been overthrown. There are no more parades, no more respect, because they have not prevented war, had not prevented evil, but had only substituted the hypocrisy of appearances to hide the reality of evil underneath. "A pretty gory carnival that had been for the last four years!" Valentine exclaims, expressing the post-war (only minutes old) world's contempt for middle-class, Victorian morality. Because of these revolutionary changes, Valentine can become Tietjens' mistress when only a few years before she could not.

Valentine remembers the night ride in the dog-cart, linking this novel with *Some Do Not.* . . . While the remembrance itself is not obscure, the full impact of the memory certainly depends on our having read the first volume of the tetralogy. The context of Valentine's recalling of that scene six years before is one of cynical remembrance on her part of her youthful romanticizing. And her rather cold, detached view of her relationship with Tietjens is in direct contrast to the sympathetic rendering of that romantic, idyllic though illusory, mist-enshrouded episode in *Some Do Not.* . . .

Without having read *Some Do Not* . . . and *No More Parades,* the reader would lose the associated meanings of this motif—the catastrophe to their reputations symbolized by the accident (here only barely mentioned as an item of objective reporting), the sound of the crash paralleling that of artillery shells in the war, Tietjens' concern for the bleeding horse foreshadowing his guilt feelings over the death of O Nine Morgan, and the mist image with its obscuring of reality becoming transformed into the mud image which dominates the middle section of this third volume. The reader would not even know, not having read the other two volumes, that it is Tietjens being referred to here since his name is not mentioned until near the end of the first part.

Furthermore, Valentine's referring to Tietjens as "it" foreshadows the more extended use of this device in *The Last Post,* thus making clear the significance of Sylvia's being thought of as "It" in Valentine's mind. Valentine has not been in communication with Tietjens even by letter since he left for France (the end of *Some Do Not* . . .). He is in a sense "dead" to her, not only because he is a soldier and she a pacifist, but also because their relationship is untenable (he cannot marry her, and she will not become his mistress). To speak his name is to admit him back into her life. Paradoxically, not to speak his name is to keep him alive; the name taboo was a powerful one in primitive societies since it prevented one's enemies from harming one as long as one's identity remained secret.

Sylvia is "It" to Valentine because she does not belong to the

world of peace; her attempt to continue the war, to pursue the
enemy into his own territory (as Mark Tietjens wanted the Allies
to pursue the Germans), is doomed to failure because the world
is sick of war; or, rather, the war itself becomes the sickness it
was supposed to cure (witness Mark's paralysis of withdrawal
because the Allies would not pursue a policy of total "victory").
Sylvia surrenders to Valentine by surrendering her identity as
Mrs. Tietjens to Valentine.

The essential importance of *Parade's End* as a multiple novel
is, therefore, that, though the separate novels can be read as
separate entities, the tetralogy as a literary form is greater than
its four parts because these interlocking motifs expand the meaning of the whole. We have already pointed out that the "no more
parade" motif is echoed in the "no more respect" theme of post-
war rebellion against tradition, thus expanding the meaning of
that motif. At the beginning of Part Two of *A Man Could Stand
Up—*, which takes us back to the time (April, 1918) when
Tietjens is at the front in the trenches, the title motif is suggested
indirectly by the recurring, almost mystical illusion Tietjens has
that if his body were suspended by a process of levitation so
that "his head were level with a particular splash of purposeless
whitewash [. . .] he would be in an inviolable sphere" (543).

The "inviolable sphere" is of course an illusion, for at the front
line there is none; however, the trenches provided an illusion of
one as long as a man did not stand up and expose his body above
the protective level. This illusory sense of inviolability is reinforced by its relationship to the mist image in *Some Do Not . . .* :
the mist-enshrouded dog-cart ride was a romantic illusion, for
peace itself was one; the pre-war period of complacent peace
obscured the inevitable collision of nations, and Tietjens' romanticizing of his relationship with Valentine obscured the
reality of their situation, Sylvia already having declared war on
Tietjens. Therefore, the ironic meaning of the motif, a man could
stand up, is reinforced; it is not, however, until the final novel
of the tetralogy that the full irony of the motif is revealed.

Nonetheless, the irony of the motif is implicit in the time shift
from peacetime to wartime in these first two parts of *A Man
Could Stand Up—*, just as irony is found in the illusion of "peace
in our time" in the first part of *Some Do Not . . .* by its contrast
with part two. The motif is first stated by the Lincolnshire ser-

geant at the moment Tietjens is thinking about Perowne being killed, buried in the mud of the trenches, a smile on his face: "You want to stand up! Take a look around [. . . .] Like as if you wanted to breathe deep after bein' in a stoopin' posture for a long time!" (570). The irony is in the foreshadowing of Tietjens' standing up out of the trenches to "take a look around," for, like Perowne, he is buried in the mud. "A man could stand up," as Tietjens himself understood the sergeant, means peace; for only then is a man free to stand up on a hill without fear.

Tietjens' real fear is that he might go mad; it is not a fear of death (there is even a suggestion of a death-wish in his standing up out of the trenches), but that the physical shock of a wound would trigger madness, as being shell-shocked earlier had partially affected his memory. Hemingway in *The Sun Also Rises* symbolizes the mental shock of war through Jake Barnes's emasculation. Ford's approach is closer to Virginia Woolf's in *Mrs. Dalloway*: Septimus Warren Smith's fear is that he is unable to feel, that his emotions had been killed by the war. Ford stresses the emotions intensified by the war, rather than the physical suffering.

Tietjens says at the end of *No More Parades*, "Everyone who has served in this war will be a marked man for a long time after it is over" (490). The psychic wounds take longer to heal than the physical. Valentine comes to understand that "the dreadful thing about the whole war was that [. . .] the suffering had been [. . .] mental rather than physical" (659). Tietjens himself, though he had had pneumonia, admits that his hospitalization was more for mental than physical reasons. Aranjuez, who has lost his eye, is without bitterness; and he praises Tietjens for saving his life, as though the physical suffering of losing his eye purged him of mental torture. It is Tietjens who is mentally tortured by the thought that he is responsible for the loss of Aranjuez's eye.

In contrast to Aranjuez, McKechnie, physically unwounded, has gone mad; his paranoaic sense of persecution drives him to accuse Tietjens of selling his wife to General Campion in order to get his promotion (he was convinced that he should have been given command of the battalion, not Tietjens). McKechnie presents an important contrast to Tietjens because his situation is similar: he refuses to divorce his wife on principle, and goes about with his wife and her lover to protect her reputation. However, McKechnie lacks the personal integrity and inner reserve by which he can survive the disgrace of being dismissed from the army. He can only blame others for his disgrace. Paradoxically, Tietjens survives because, though much of his mental suffering is caused by others, he is able to accept the responsibility for his actions and his principles.

Tietjens survives because he receives his baptism of mud. For the first time, half-buried in the mud, he realizes he must save himself before he can save others. This realization foreshadows his willingness to salvage his life by living with Valentine; the other way, to continue to struggle against the mud, is to be sucked up in it, in McKechnie's madness. The situation suggests Stein's answer in *Lord Jim* to the question of how to live: "In the destructive element immerse." This solution is not without risks—Tietjens is "strafed" by General Campion for appearing "on parade" covered with mud, and Sylvia still seeks to destroy him—but the destructive element will buoy him up. Tietjens, who has a "passionate Tory sense of freedom," is free to stand up; but he will never be completely free of the mud.

Tietjens and Valentine are reunited at the end of *A Man Could Stand Up—*, in a happy but not sentimental ending. There is still the problem of Sylvia, and Tietjens is still plagued with the accusation of immorality. Valentine senses that their reunion has nothing to do with conscience: "one is urged by blind destiny!" (654). The enemy was fear, not society; and Tietjens is at last free to make his own way in a world where "a man could now stand up on a hill" (668). Valentine and Tietjens have come full circle. At the end of *Some Do Not* . . . they had separated, seemingly "forever"; at the end of *A Man Could Stand Up—*, "they would be alone together now. For ever!" (669). The last post has sounded, the soldiers are quartered for the night, and the war is over. However, life is not over, and mental tensions cannot be resolved so neatly: "Men might stand up on hills but the mental torture could not be expelled" (660). That the mental suffering could not be expelled by the declaration of an armistice is a clue to the continuation of Sylvia's war after peace is declared. *The Last Post* is the parallel portrait of Armistice Day in Sylvia's war, just as *A Man Could Stand Up—* is the rendering of the historical date when Valentine and Tietjens declare their separate peace with the enemies of their happiness: fear, repression, denial, renunciation, self-sacrifice.

VI   The Last Post

At first glance *The Last Post* seems quite different in narrative pattern from the other three novels of the tetralogy: Mark Tietjens is the focal narrating consciousness although he appears in only one major scene in *Some Do Not . . .* and none in the other two novels. Furthermore, four characters—Marie-Léonie, Cramp, Mrs. de Bray Pape, and Mark Tietjens, Jr.—all of whom we meet directly for the first time, are also narrating consciousnesses but are subordinate in their narrative roles. These differences tend to obscure the interrelatedness of *The Last Post* with the rest of the tetralogy.

Cross-references to earlier scenes and motifs, partially explained motivations which make sense only within the full perspective of the accumulated character portrayals in the tetralogy as a whole, parallels and contrasts in characters, scenes and themes which can only be fully understood in conjunction with the other three novels—all contribute to the dependence of one's understanding of this last novel on one's having read the rest of the tetralogy. But the obverse question remains of whether or not *The Last Post* is essential to the meaning of the other three novels; if not, then *Parade's End* is unsuccessful as a multiple novel. The multiple novel as a literary form must be unified to be successful: it must present a composite whole rather than a series of related but separate works.

In the dedicatory letter to *No More Parades* Ford states his intentions concerning the development of the tetralogy: "*Some Do Not . . .*—of which this one [*No More Parades*] is not so much a continuation as a reinforcement—showed you the Tory at home during war-time; this shows you the Tory going up the line. If I am vouchsafed health and intelligence for long enough I propose to show you the same man in the line [*A Man Could Stand Up—*] and in process of being re-constructed [*The Last Post*]" (vii-viii).

Whatever Ford's original intention, *The Last Post* does not show Tietjens being reconstructed in the sense of being spiritually reborn: he is openly living with Valentine, something which they would not do on principle all through the war. Because he will not accept responsibility for Groby, he renounces his inheritance and heritage, even though he and Valentine are nearly destitute. The reconstruction of Tietjens is instead a devastating image of the new, post-war modern man, symbolized by his airplane trip in direct contrast to the pre-war, dog-cart ride of *Some Do Not* . . . which had ended in violent collision with that symbol of change and modernity, the automobile.

Tietjens as a Tory adhering to an eighteenth-century ethic is dead; the new, reconstructed man survives precisely because he has come to terms with his times and has rejected moral principles and social responsibilities. Sylvia is defeated not so much because she has been regenerated but because Tietjens has adapted himself to the modern world and is therefore much less vulnerable to her machinations; what does it avail her to have Groby Great Tree cut down when he will have nothing to do with the estate. Tietjens needed no spiritual reformation, for he had maintained his integrity throughout the war; his transformation is the opposite, a materialistic and bodily regeneration which suits the times. The apotheosis of his reconstruction is that he should earn his living, however poorly, by selling the material remnants of the dead past, his now dead heritage, eighteenth-century furniture.

Therefore, the developmental pattern of *Parade's End* is consistent in its irony; and the culminating irony revealed in *The Last Post* is essential to understanding the whole design. Mark Tietjens, Jr., inherits Groby; and, though he may resemble Christopher Tietjens physically, he is the opposite of all that Tietjens stood for as a Tory. Young Mark is opposed to the peasant-like way of life that Christopher and Mark Tietjens have adopted; to him, "This was an industrial age. The peasant had always spoilt every advance in the ideas of the world" (712). He is attracted to Marxian-Communism; and, although he is largely aping the ideas of his social set at Cambridge (a set which includes the Prime Minister's son and General Campion's nephew —Campion who nearly had apoplexy when Sylvia told him Tietjens was a Socialist!), Young Mark's ideas are obviously intended by Ford to illustrate the post-war generation's revolt against the ideas and ideals of the older generation. One senses that young Mark is used by Ford to *reflect* the post-war revolution rather than *be* it. Although young Mark insists, along with his Cambridge set, that he believes in free love and all that, he is actually quite conventional, even Victorian, in his attitude toward Valentine as a Bad Woman with Advanced Views. Even his reason for wanting Groby Great Tree cut down merely reflects the up-to-date idea that it is "unsanitary"; it does not arise out of any deep inner conviction, symbolic or otherwise, such as Sylvia's does.

Young Mark is Christopher's double—he is an instinctive Tory without the social and intellectual milieu to give it meaning. It is *passé* in his set to be a Tory, and therefore he can only ape the current ideas of his generation without being a true rebel. His deepest instincts are a love of the land—"a lovely glimpse under the trees. . . . That's England"—yet consciously he can only repeat what others say: "a house overhung by trees is unsanitary." His innate Toryism withers and dies because it is not nurtured by traditions. He inherits Groby, but there is doubt whether he is a Tietjens.

This doubt is not resolved by Mark Tietjens' sentimental identification at the end. Sylvia, the only person who could know who the father was, prefers to call young Mark by his first name, Michael; and, while she does so because she hates Mark Tietjens, there is also the possibility that she does it because she knows Christopher is not the father. There is even more doubt that Sylvia knows because she had pre-marital relations with both Tietjens and Drake. Ultimately, the answer remains ambiguous; but it does not matter since what is important is that young Mark inherits Groby. The question of who shall inherit Groby is, as in E. M. Forster's *Howards End*, that of who shall inherit England. While Forster makes it clear that it is, for better or for worse, someone of mixed heritage, Helen Schlegel's bastard son, Ford uses ambiguity to achieve a similar theme: Young Mark is not Tietjens' spiritual heir even if we assume he is a Tietjens; the irony is that innately he could have been Tietjens' spiritual heir even if we assume he is Drake's son; but Tietjens' kind of Toryism is extinct and there are no heirs. The new generation takes over, for better or for worse; but it is without roots because it must destroy the old (symbolized by Groby Great Tree) in order to inherit the earth. It should be clear, however, that Ford does not place the onus on the new generation; the old order destroyed itself because it was incapable of harmony of body and soul. There is, however, little hope for the future in the dis-harmony between young Mark's professed ideas and his sup-pressed heritage.

Mark Tietjens is also Christopher's "double," revealing another aspect of man's essential dualism. While Christopher makes his peace with the new order, Mark, still at war with his times, re-fuses to make the adjustment to the post-war world. Like Sylvia, who seeks to continue her war with Tietjens, Mark wanted to continue the war with the Germans; but, since he is unable to change the course of history, he will try to keep himself "pure" and "guiltless" by withdrawing from the world into complete isolation. He will not "speak a word nor stir a finger" because of his disillusionment; he will blame "all the calamities of the world" on the terms of peace. His physical illness is real, but his withdrawal is a spiritual illness, a perversion of the mind.

Like D. H. Lawrence, Ford suggests through Mark Tietjens that an over-developed intellectuality is the modern sin; his body is "dead" (paralyzed), only his eyes are alive (the windows of his soul), but his mind is very active and alive, justifying Tiet-jens' ways to God. The opening paragraph of Lawrence's *Lady Chatterley's Lover* could well serve as the theme of *The Last Post*: "Ours is essentially a tragic age, so we refuse to take it tragically. The cataclysm has happened, we are among the ruins, we start to build up new little habits, to have new little hopes. It is rather hard work: there is now no smooth road into the future: but we go round, or scramble over the obstacles. We've got to live, no matter how many skies have fallen."[8] Christopher and Valentine (and the rest of the world) refuse to take the situation tragically and start to build up new little habits and hopes among the ruins. No matter how many "shower strings" Sylvia pulls, they go on living, surviving "the Flood." Because Mark and Sylvia want to view it tragically, he dies and she is defeated.

Christopher's refusal to use his brains in the service of war saves him from Mark's paralysis of the will to live. Mark, having over-developed his mind in the service of war, which led him to view war and victory as simply a matter of superiority in trans-portation, has lost perspective and a sense of proportion in the post-war world. Though he believes "a man is in the world to do his duty by his nation and his family" (736) and though he

believes the world needs to return to the old standards of common sense and probity, he himself "was finished with the world."

Applying the same process of logical reasoning to Christopher's
problems as he applied to the logistics of transport during the
war, Mark Tietjens arrives at mutually contradictory solutions,
both of them rational in their logic. Starting from the premise
that their father committed suicide over the scandals about
Christopher, Mark comes to the conclusion that Valentine was
their father's illegitimate daughter and therefore Tietjens, Sr.,
committed suicide because Christopher was having an incestuous
relationship with Valentine. Starting from the opposite premise
that their father's death was an accident, Mark comes to the conclusion that Tietjens, Sr., a sentimental gentleman who would
mercifully put a wounded rabbit out of its agony as soon as
possible, accidentally shot himself as he crawled through the
hedge on such a mission and that, therefore, Valentine is not an
illegitimate child. She and Christopher can live happily together
because *their* illegitimate child is not the result of an incestuous
relationship, and indeed Christopher need not even feel guilty,
thinking he had caused his father's suicide!

A heaven of happiness or a hell of human misery is created
depending on which premise is used, on which set of appearances is taken as the truth. Ford forcibly underscores his theme
of the discrepancy between appearances and reality—man will
create his vision of reality from appearances and then these
themselves become the reality for him. Mark himself states the
discrepancy, after he has decided the curse is off the family and
all's right with the world, "you must have a pattern to interpret
things by" (832). And Sylvia comes to realize that her success
in getting other men to believe what she tells them about Christopher rests on her being a beautiful woman: "Beauty and truth
have a way of appearing to be akin [. . .]" (786).

Sylvia's false stories about Tietjens are at least motivated by
hatred and sexual jealousy which fit into an allegorical framework (Perowne in *No More Parades* calls her La Belle Dame
Sans Merci). Ironically, Mark is motivated by the best of intentions toward Christopher; the two brothers had become "as thick
as thieves" during those three weeks before Armistice, and at the
end Mark gives Christopher his benediction; "A good man!" he
tells Valentine. Yet in his mind only hours before his death, Mark

had condemned his brother to a hell on earth. It is not that we are to be left with an alternative of suicide and incest on the one hand and the sentimental optimism that God's in His Heaven all's right with the world on the other. Mark Tietjens *invented* the incest explanation to begin with on no better evidence than that on which he dismisses it.

One senses throughout *Parade's End* that the human condition is to suffer self-created agonies—the false gossip about Christopher, the mental sufferings of the war, Sylvia's own agony of flesh and spirit, Mark's self-isolation. The real irony is that all the mental anguish may have been for nothing more real than misinterpreted appearances. In the instance of Christopher's suffering because of gossip, the double irony is that it is just as easy and just as right or wrong to explain things optimistically or pessimistically, sentimentally or cynically, as Mark Tietjens demonstrates in *The Last Post*. The war itself may have been fought to feed the private vanities of those in power, just as Sylvia's private war was fought to satiate hers. What finally changes is not the human condition but the interpretation: to young Mark the post-war world is one of material progress (paralleling the train symbol that begins the tetralogy); to Mark senior it is one of degeneracy and depravity; to Sylvia it is a hostile world in which she is alienated, and to Valentine and Christopher it is a world of truce with the past so that they can survive in the present and begin building for the future. The past is dead; the future will be what man chooses to make of it.

The last post motif sounds the death knell of the past. It is primarily associated with Mark Tietjens, whose thoughts are of the past that for him ended on Armistice Day. The first reference to the motif occurs when Mark recalls having heard the tattoo sounded as part of the victory celebration on Armistice Day, but to Mark it represents "the last of England," the end of his world since he will not take part in the future. Groby itself is associated with the motif, for both Mark and Christopher have renounced their claim to it; and, since there is doubt that young Mark is a Tietjens, Groby will pass out of Tietjens' hands (foreshadowed by the fact that it is now being rented by the American woman, Mrs. de Bray Pape, who wants Groby Great Tree cut down). The cutting down of the tree reinforces the motif, for "Groby Great Tree was the symbol of Tietjens" (733). Ultimately, the last post motif is associated with Mark Tietjens' death, for it is played for the dead; in a flashback to Armistice Day, Mark tells Valentine: "you may play the Last Post, for me," (775) for Mark "died" on that day. Just before he dies, Mark Tietjens composes his own epitaph, *"Here lies one whose name was writ in sea-birds!"* (832). Christopher returns and tells Mark, "I found your case of sea-birds thrown on a rubble heap," and Mark thinks bitterly: "It was as well that one's services were unforgettable!" (835). The end of all he stood for and his own death coincide. In this context the culminating irony of the novel must be understood. When Mark attempts to tell the apocryphal story of the Yorkshireman and the Flood to Valentine, he cannot articulate it because her world has nothing to do with his. "It's bound to clear up!": life goes on, but the good of the past is buried with the bad; each generation collects its own case of sea-birds, and each new world throws the old on the rubble heap.

Part One of *The Last Post* ends with the refrain, "But one must adapt oneself to one's day; the times were changed" (778)— advice Mark does not heed. Part Two begins with Sylvia's being aware that "times changed, the world changed," foreshadowing her defeat at the end; but she (unlike Mark) attempts to continue the war, unwilling to withdraw from life. She is fighting for her life; the last post is not yet for her. But the world, sick of war, will no longer tolerate her pursuit of the enemy, no more than it would have tolerated continuing the war against the Germans by pursuing them into Germany. She is defeated because the world is at peace: "Her main bitterness was that they had this peace," and thus she recognizes that "her world was waning" (808) because it is a world that thrives on emotional tensions. She can only triumph by making Christopher and Valentine suffer, but they are now invulnerable to her machinations. She surrenders to Valentine, not because she is regenerated, but because, like Mark, she represents the past which is dead and because Valentine, pregnant with Christopher's child, belongs to the future.

Mark Tietjens recalls near the end of Part One what he had said to Valentine on Armistice Day, some of the last words he spoke before his self-willed silence: "make it your world and it may go to rack and ruin how it will. I am done with it. But then . . . do you accept the responsibility!" (775). Valentine accepts the responsibility, but she lacks faith in the future: "How are we to live? How are we ever to live?" she sobs to Mark (835). Coming full circle, Mark breaks his silence and tells her Christopher is "a good man," providing Valentine with the needed faith to go on. She will not tell Marie-Léonie, Mark's wife, of his last words because "she did not need them as much as I." These are the last words of the novel, and thus the tetralogy ends on a hopeful note. The last post has sounded, the war is over, peace has come. But with parade's end comes the end of the way of life symbolized at the beginning of *Parade's End* by the "perfectly appointed railway carriage," which received its unexpected jolt (the war), and by the cutting down of Groby Great Tree.

CHAPTER 5

"Last Post": Ford's Final Novels

THE five novels Ford published after the completion of
Parade's End form a continuation rather than a development
of the themes and techniques found in his earlier novels. The
same techniques used so successfully in *The Good Soldier* and
in *Parade's End* are also employed in these last novels—time-shift,
progression d'effet, impressionism. Themes that Ford developed
in his earlier novels are also stated in these final ones—the discrepancy between appearance and reality, the double motif, the
reconstruction of the disillusioned protagonist. But this last phase
of Ford's career as a novelist is an anti-climax since the five
novels are in themselves lesser works. Coming as they do after
the great achievement of *The Good Soldier* and *Parade's End,*
they are an even greater disappointment to the reader who has
followed the development of Ford's craftsmanship from the early
novels to the masterpieces.

One reason the last novels are an anti-climax is that the first
of them, *A Little Less Than Gods*, and the last, *Vive Le Roy*, are
slight. Ford, one senses, was a restless writer; he always had
to have something going, whatever it was, serious or slight,
monumental or small. Characteristically, in this last period he
managed to publish besides five novels, a semi-fictional auto-
biography, *No Enemy* (1929); a history of *The English Novel*
(1929); the two autobiographical reminiscences, *Return to Yesterday* (1931) and *It Was the Nightingale* (1933); the essay
volumes *Provence* (1935) and *Great Trade Route* (1937); *Collected Poems* (1936); a volume of memories and criticisms,
Portraits from Life (1937); a history of literature from Confucius to the present, *The March of Literature* (1938); and he
was working on another novel when he died in 1939. Such pro-
lific output, in spite of Ford's prodigious energy, explains in part
why Ford could write such inferior novels as *A Little Less Than*

Gods and *Vive Le Roy*, and why his last novels, while technically competent, lack the artistic control and tightness of structure of his masterpieces. Even the best of the five, *The Rash Act* and *Henry for Hugh*, fail because of loose structural control.

I A Little Less Than Gods

A Little Less Than Gods (1928), though published in the same year as *The Last Post* (1928), was written after its publication. It is understandable that Ford, after the major effort of the tetralogy, would turn to material readily at hand: the Napoleonic tale which he and Conrad had originally considered for collaboration and which Conrad had begun writing as a separate novel, entitled *Suspense*, shortly before his death but had never completed. Since Conrad had not completed his independent version of this material, Ford, as he indicates in the prefatory letter to *A Little Less Than Gods*, felt at liberty to use it.[1]

A Little Less Than Gods, Ford's last historical novel, uses the background of Napeoleon's triumphant return to France from Elba and his eventual defeat. The main theme is simply that great heroes wreck worlds and human lives in their something less than god-like omnipotence as demi-gods. The invincible Napoleon is defeated; the victorious Wellington is debased by money; the wealthy Assheton Smith, who "is for all Europe the glass of fashion and the model for *ton*," is a vain and arrogant man, "whose money is his sole means of illustriousness and whose heart is as dry and thin as last year's leaf"; the powerful, autocratic Tsar Alexander is ruled by his passion for his mistress; the heroic soldier Marshall Ney unheroically disguises himself as a woman to escape execution. Only the wealthy financier, Baron de Fréjus, achieves heroism by substituting himself for Marshall Ney and dying before a firing squad; but the Baron is motivated by personal cynicism. The theme is intensified by the romantic idealizing of these demi-gods by protagonist George Feilding, whose disillusionment heralds the end of a heroic age that existed mainly in his romanticizing attitudes and was as sham as the duel he fought at the beginning of the novel with the swashbuckling Colonel Count dei Gatti Vivario, the Corsican hero who by the end of the novel, stripped of his honors, is plain Mr. Gatti.

The anti-heroic theme of *A Little Less Than Gods* should be seen in relation to the post-war debunking of history and the glories of war, but it should also be seen as an extension of the theme Ford had developed in *Parade's End*: no more parades finds its echo in Hélène de Fréjus' sounding the death knell of the Napoleonic era: "And now . . . all gone. All that glory. All those demi-gods." *No Enemy*, subtitled *A Tale of Reconstruction*, further expands and explains the theme of post-war personal reconstruction in peace through the love of nature that is a source of strength in Mark and Christopher Tietjens in *The Last Post*. In *No Enemy* the poet Gringoire, Ford's alter ego, achieves peace within himself through love of the land, just as he had found moments of peace during the war by awareness of landscapes.

But for Feilding there is no "reconstruction," only disillusionment. His great heroes have become less than gods, and his great romantic love for Hélène, an incestuous one since he discovers that she is his half-sister. Denied his heroes, he is left with a forbidden love, having earlier rejected Princess Pauline who loves him. But Assheton Smith, the richest man in the world, survives and is triumphant in the end. "Neither the Redeemer nor anti-Christ," he symbolizes the triumph of moneyed power over the heroic, Napoleonic gestures and the romantic ideals of honor and valor. Baron de Fréjus' sacrificial death represents the victory of wealth over soldierly valor, for the wealthy financier has replaced the public hero, Marshall Ney, as his double. The motif of the double—already noted in *The Good Soldier* and *Parade's End*—is also developed by Ford in his next novel, *When the Wicked Man* (1931).

II   When the Wicked Man

In *When the Wicked Man* the motif of the double is based on the occult phenomenon found in German folklore: the *doppelgänger*, the supposed ghost of a living person which appears in times of emotional stress. And indeed Notterdam, the protagonist, remembers having read as a boy a story "of a man who had been haunted by a double of himself called a '*dopplegaenger*.' The appearance of the double had always presaged disaster of a hideous nature. Finally he had fired a pistol through the double's heart—to see that he had fractured a mirror and to fall dead."[2] The thematic purpose is the same as in the earlier novels: self-recognition.

However, the *dopplegänger* motif in *When the Wicked Man* suggests not only Notterdam's conscience but the psychological deterioration of his personality: he is haunted by his *dopplegänger* in moments "of extreme depression, fatigue or alcoholic indulgence." Ford's interest, nonetheless, is neither in psychological or in occult aberrations; the occult (Notterdam's ancestral double is the sixteenth-century French astrologer Nostradamus, originally Michel de Notre-Dame) is used by Ford to reflect the moral aberrations of the business world that his characters inhabit.

Notterdam, though a book publisher, dislikes books and authors; he reneges on a book contract (admittedly signed when he was drunk) and drives Porter, a young novelist, to suicide. Notterdam and his future mistress, Henrietta Felise, cover up the circumstances so that the death is declared accidental. The publishing firm profits from the posthumous publication of Porter's works. Yet Notterdam, a man plagued by his conscience, is not so evil as his business partner Kratch, whose ego must be fed with business triumphs or else he will die of his symbolic sickness (to please Kratch, Notterdam reneges on the Porter contract). Kratch has cuckolded Notterdam for years while Notterdam seeks an honorable solution by divorcing Elspeth and marrying Henrietta. And Lola Porter, the "bereaved" widow, preys on Notterdam; her extortions of money are matched by the contortions of her hysteria as she deteriorates psychologically.

Notterdam's attempt to reform is ironically thwarted. In a scene that is a mixture of psychological fantasy and realism, Notterdam goes berserk and shoots his "double," attempting to kill his evil self; in actuality, he kills the notorious gangster, McKeown, who has been besieging Lola Porter to give him money. Symbolically, Notterdam has killed his soul; for now he is a national hero who can never tell the truth about himself. Thus the title, taken from the Bible, is ironic: "when the wicked man turneth away from his wickedness . . . he shall save his soul alive." What Notterdam "saves" is the public image of himself as a moral man of "spotless rectitude" (he has caused Porter's death), a businessman of integrity (his firm is engaged in brib-

ing politicians), and a hero who had saved the life of a beautiful
woman (he had almost raped her) by killing a wicked man (his
killing McKeown is the accidental result of a hallucination).

The dark forest of his heart remains hidden because he is
now more than ever captive of the social mores of the time and
the false legend of his heroism. The truth about himself is
summarized:

> His work was useless as an educational edifice; he was carrying it
> on by means of political corruption: in the eyes of decent people he
> had stolen from his rivals products that their energy and discernment
> had helped them to discover. He had, in effect, murdered a remark-
> able contemporary figure; he was so weak that he had on his hands
> a woman who was doing a good deal of harm to his reputation. His
> wife for years had been unfaithful to him so that he was cuckolded
> [. . .] He had been a dull husband, having gradually become obese,
> slow, dumb. He had never gained any of the shining triumphs that
> should make a woman regard you as a hero (304).

But the public does not want heroes to be unheroic, and the
wicked man who hides his transgressions "shall surely live, he
shall not die." Thus, as in *The Good Soldier*, the microcosm of
private transgressions becomes the macrocosm of public transgressions.

III   The Rash Act *and* Henry For Hugh

The Rash Act (1933) and *Henry for Hugh* (1934) should be
read as a single novel, for the second is a sequel. The two-part
novel fails, however, for it lacks the cohesiveness of the structural interrelationship necessary to the multiple novel form.
Henry for Hugh, as the sequel, not only dissipates rather than
fulfills the promise of the first volume, but suffers from the weakness of many sequels published separately: needless repetition
of antecedent action which, in spite of Ford's use of the time
shift, does not sufficiently intensify character revelation or ade-
quately reinforce recurring images and symbols. Such weakness
in the sequel was perhaps inevitable because of Ford's intention
in this second volume: the reconstruction of a passive character
who, like Mark Tietjens, is physically and emotionally im-
mobilized.

Both *The Rash Act* and *Henry for Hugh* are the most direct, literal statements of the *dopplegänger* motif: Henry Martin Aluin Smith assumes the identity and life of his double, Hugh Monckton Allard Smith. Henry Martin, an American ne'er-do-well, has decided to commit suicide; his life is a failure by modern society's materialistic standards of success, symbolized by his father, a self-made man, whose candy business is a success. Hugh Monckton, a wealthy Englishman and successful businessman, has also decided to commit suicide on the same day because he is a failure in love; his mistress Gloria Malmstrom (the maelstrom of his emotions) has rejected him and decided to return to her husband. Henry "fails" in his attempt to commit suicide (literally, "the rash act"), but Hugh "succeeds."

Henry commits his "rash act" by impulsively substituting his identity cards for Hugh's when he accidentally comes across his double's body, thus "killing" Henry Martin and "resurrecting" Hugh Monckton, whose body is buried as Henry Martin's. Although the interchange of identities is effected on a literal and realistic level, the double motif is intended as a fable: Henry's failure to commit suicide is no mere muddlement; while he has a purpose in life, he cannot kill himself; and his commitment to saving the boat (personified as a woman) in the storm is one to life. Love is the saving grace, and Henry saves himself because he has loved.

Henry is seriously injured when the boat crashes in spite of his efforts, but then his soul has been sick. Through the use of a series of time shifts in *The Rash Act*, the past life of Henry Martin is revealed—his hatred of his father, his failure in the world of business and finance, his successful conquests of women without any permanent relationships. As a drowning man supposedly reviews his life in the last moments before dying, so does Henry see his life in the last hours and decides that his life has been uneventful and that "he had never given pleasure" because "passion . . . was not for him or for his day." He envies the seemingly happy Hugh Monckton, who gives pleasure, and wishes he were him, thinking that money makes all the difference. But, when he takes over the identity of Hugh, he realizes that money makes no difference. He learns that Hugh's soul has also been sick.

Landscape is the recuperative power and love is the regenerative power. In *Provence* and in *Great Trade Route* Ford celebrates the Mediterranean way of life with its pacifying effect of climate and food on the character in contrast to the belligerent Nordic North with its cold, gray climate and indigestible food. Ford, a self-exile from post-war England, himself had lived in the Provence in the 1920's and 1930's when he was not in Paris or New York. Provence is the setting of *Henry for Hugh* and its sunny climate helps Henry recover physically and psychologically from his wounds.

However, Ford does not present his theme in such over-simplified and exaggerated terms as he does in the didactic *Provence* and *Great Trade Route*. Henry, as was Hugh, is an Anglo-Saxon; and he would like to be an influence for good on others—but the warm, sunny climate so appeals to his passive nature that he tends to vegetate. It becomes his means of escape from the world and from responsibility. It is true he is under doctor's orders not to excite himself and is thus forbidden sexual passion, but his impotence is a symbol of his soul's sickness and of the world's (the depression). This passivity of the protagonist contributes largely to the lack of dramatic tension in *Henry for Hugh*.

It is through Eudoxie's love that Henry recovers his soul and is spiritually regenerated. She finds her own salvation in loving Henry and seeks to save him through her love. She not only shares with Henry the secret of his assumption of Hugh's identity, but insists that he continue the deception for the good of others who depend on him, and for the good of the country, which depends on the Monckton automobile company (a symbol of solvency in the midst of world depression). Eudoxie thus states the main theme of this two-part novel: renunciation of self-identity, not through the nihilistic negation of suicide but through accepting new responsibilities, is the highest form of abnegation. During the early months of his role as Hugh, Henry had feared the loss of his own identity; at the end, though regretting the loss of his peaceful existence without responsibilities, he accepts an active role in life as Hugh and achieves the goal he had desired but never had reached in his identity as Henry Martin: giving pleasure to others.

Ford, the historian of the breakdown of Victorian and Edwardian civilization in *The Good Soldier* and in *Parade's End*, was concerned with the illnesses of post-war civilization. His last novels are set against a background of social and economic up-

heaval, and even his historical novel, *A Little Less Than Gods,*
suggests that the Napoleonic wars were the end of a heroic age
that contained within it the seeds of its own destruction through
the rise to power of the capitalists. *The Rash Act* and *Henry for
Hugh* have as their setting the depression, a world on the brink
of revolutions, panics, disasters, even war. Henry's illness reflects in microcosm that of the world at large; and Hugh suffered from severe headaches, as a result of a war wound, a
contributing factor to his suicide. Macdonald, Hugh's secretary
and a dedicated Communist, hates Henry as a symbol of world
capitalism; and Jeanne Becquerel, a Communist whom Henry
had saved from an attempted suicide over the death of Hugh,
marries Macdonald and joins him in his determination to expose
Henry as an impostor. Macdonald's fanatic hate provides a
thematic contrast to the unselfish love of Eudoxie, the dark girl
(in contrast to Jeanne's pale whiteness); but even Eudoxie is not
a symbol of purity: she has been a loose woman and a drug
addict in her defiance of authority and tradition. Henry considered himself one of the lost generation: his marriage a failure,
childless and meaningless; his one attempt at writing made into
a book of cheap pornography by an unscrupulous publisher; his
war experiences uneventful but disillusioning; and his feeling of
not belonging to the times a contributing factor to his decision
to commit suicide. This sense of personal and social crisis in the
characters reinforces the theme of the regenerative power of love
and the need for accepting the responsibility of life within
society.

IV Vive Le Roy

Vive Le Roy (1936), Ford's last published novel, provides an
interesting footnote to the motifs of the double and of the social
and economic upheaval of the 1930's. A frankly melodramatic
treatment of themes more seriously treated earlier, *Vive Le Roy*
uses as its setting a fabled civil war in France between the Communists and the Royalists in the 1930's, the Royalists themselves
divided between the benevolent feudalism of an Henri V and
the Fascist adherents of the Queen. The Royalists have triumphed, but the king has been assassinated. Monsieur de la
Penthièvre, an important Royalist advisor, notices the close physical resemblance to the king of a young American doctor, Walter

Leroy, who, out of vague Communist leanings and strong anti-Royalist feelings, is amateurishly acting as an agent for American Communists to deliver money to the French Communists. Kidnapped, Leroy is forced to stand in for *le roi*, but by the end Leroy has willingly assumed the role, presumably out of a sense of duty and responsibility to help maintain stability and authority in the French government and apparently out of the conviction that the Royalists, not the revolutionists of the left and the right, will best serve the utopian ideal of small agricultural communities under a benevolent monarch.

Complete with an international detective, Penkethman, who turns out to be Leroy's father, *Vive Le Roy* cannot be taken seriously as either political criticism or detective story; and perhaps part of the difficulty is that Ford seemed undecided which direction his novel should take. It is difficult to believe in Leroy's "conversion" to the Royalist cause, rendered as it is at second-hand by Penkethman and Cassie Mathers, Leroy's beloved. It is even more difficult to accept the political theory of feudalistic agrarianism under an absolute but benevolent monarch on which Leroy's conversion rests, portrayed as it is against the background of the Communist and Fascist revolutions of the 1930's, that are over-simplified to the point of naïve absurdity. As a suspense story *Vive Le Roy* is also disappointing, for the double motif is crudely contrived; and it is apparent from the beginning that M. de la Penthièvre's plan is to substitute Leroy for *le roi* because of the striking physical resemblance. But, in order to keep up the suspense as to whether Leroy is alive or dead, the point of view is shifted to Cassie in the second half of the novel, thus sacrificing the rendering of Leroy's political conversion on which the political theme and credibility rest. Thus, *Vive Le Roy*, Ford's last published novel, adds nothing to his treatment of the double motif or of the political theme.

V *Conclusion*

It does not do justice to Ford's literary reputation for the critic's "last post" to end on such a sour note. His editorship of the *English Review* and the *transatlantic review* was a major contribution to modern literature because of the high quality of their contents and because of the encouragement given to previously unpublished writers. His collaboration with Conrad, while it did not produce a major work, was significant in the development both of Ford as a novelist and of a theoretical framework for the impressionistic novel. Though his earliest and latest novels are all lesser works, Ford's reputation as a novelist rests solidly on the major achievements of *The Good Soldier* and *Parade's End*. These novels are masterpieces of the modern English novel and rightfully deserve a place on the shelf alongside the best of Conrad, Forster, Joyce, Woolf, Lawrence, and Huxley.

After the accomplishment of *The Good Soldier* and *Parade's End*, nothing short of a new, major breakthrough in technique or in thematic content would have constituted a climax in Ford's development as a novelist. Few novelists—Henry James and James Joyce are exceptions rather than the rule—have achieved perfect patterns of continuous development; and even Conrad, whose critical reputation is as solid as one ever is, has been viewed as having his anti-climax.[3] Perhaps, as Meixner points out, Ford's early novels are of considerable importance to the critic because they form the apprenticeship leading to the masterpieces; but, when the last novels are a decline from that achievement, the critic's interest is lessened (257). This observation is borne out by Carol Ohmann's book, which traces in detail Ford's apprenticeship in the early novels to his master craftsmanship in *The Good Soldier* and *Parade's End*, and which views Ford's last novels as an epilogue to his major phase.[4]

If Ford's career as a novelist had ended with *The Last Post*, the critic's story, as Ohmann suggests, would have a happy ending (175). But few novelists have had the happiness of their critics in mind, not even E. M. Forster, who alone of modern novelists stopped writing novels because he did not want to repeat himself. But, if Ford had given in to his feeling of disillusionment after the war, detailed in *It Was the Nightingale*, that he was finished as a novelist, there would have been no *Parade's End*. Instead, he made a new "beginning": adopting the name by which he is now known, Ford Madox Ford, he wrote the masterful Tietjens tetralogy.

Notes and References

Chapter One

1. Ford did contribute some passages to *Nostromo* when Conrad was very ill, but the work is Conrad's and not a collaboration. Ford also collaborated with Violet Hunt in writing *Zeppelin Nights* (1915), a series of historical sketches read by their author, Serapion Hunter, to a group of London intellectuals who are waiting out the nightly zeppelin raids on London during the early part of the war; the frame is obviously modeled on Boccaccio's *Decameron*. Most of the sketches were written by Ford, many of them having been previously published by him, with Violet Hunt providing the short connecting links between the sketches.

2. Ford Madox Ford, *Joseph Conrad: A Personal Remembrance* (London, 1924), p. 45.

3. *Ibid.*, pp. 180, 182. Because Ford made frequent use of ellipses in his works, my omissions from Ford's text are indicated by an ellipsis in brackets; any ellipsis not so enclosed is Ford's own.

4. Ford Madox Ford, *Return to Yesterday* (New York, 1932), p. 194.

5. Paul L. Wiley, *Novelist of Three Worlds: Ford Madox Ford* (Syracuse, 1962).

6. Ford Madox Ford, *The Shifting of the Fire* (London, 1892), p. 257.

7. Richard A. Cassell, *Ford Madox Ford: A Study of His Novels* (Baltimore, 1961), p. 126.

8. Ford Madox Ford and Joseph Conrad, *The Nature of a Crime* (Garden City, New York, 1926), p. 51.

9. Ford Madox Ford and Joseph Conrad, *Romance* (New York, 1904), p. 24.

Chapter Two

1. Ford Madox Ford, *Thus to Revisit* (London, 1921), p. 44.

2. Ford Madox Ford, *The Benefactor* (London, 1905), p. 6.

3. Ford Madox Ford, *The Fifth Queen* (New York, 1964), p. 591.

4. John A. Meixner, *Ford Madox Ford's Novels: A Critical Study* (Minneapolis, 1962), p. 48.

5. Martin Hume, *The Wives of Henry VIII* (New York, 1905), p. 366.

6. Francis Hackett, *Henry the Eighth* (Garden City, New York, 1931), p. 352.

7. Ford Madox Ford, *Mr. Apollo* (London, 1908), p. 309.

8. Ford Madox Ford, *The "Half Moon"* (London, 1909), p. vi. Ford had completed this novel by 1906 but publication was delayed to coincide with the tercentenary of Hudson's voyage.

9. Ford Madox Ford, *The Portrait* (London, 1910), pp. 306-7.

10. Ford Madox Ford, *A Call* (London, 1910), p. 18.

11. Ford Madox Ford, *The Simple Life Limited* (London, 1911), p. 120.

12. For a detailed summary of the traits of the chivalric hero, see Cassell, *op. cit.*, pp. 115-17.

13. Ford Madox Ford, *Ladies Whose Bright Eyes* (London, 1911), p. 357.

14. Ford Madox Ford, *The New Humpty-Dumpty* (London, 1912), p. 431.

Chapter Three

1. Ford Madox Ford, *England and the English* (New York, 1907), pp. 338, 339.

2. Ford Madox Ford, *The Good Soldier* (New York, 1951), p. 183.

3. Ford Madox Ford, *The March of Literature* (New York, 1938), p. 579.

4. For a more detailed discussion of the discrepancies in dates in relation to Ford's manuscript revisions of *The Good Soldier*, see Charles G. Hoffmann, "Ford's Manuscript Revisions of *The Good Soldier*," *English Literature in Transition*, IX, 3 (1966), 145-52.

5. Bergson's major works—*Time and Free Will, Matter and Memory*, and *Creative Evolution*—had been translated into English by 1911. Whether Ford had read any of Bergson's works, either in English or in the original French (he could read it as easily as English) before he began writing *The Good Soldier* is not known, but undoubtedly he was aware of Bergson's theories of time and memory as part of the intellectual milieu of his time.

6. See Ambrose Gordon, Jr., *The Invisible Tent: The War Novels of Ford Madox Ford* (Austin, Texas, 1964), pp. 55-7. Mr. Gordon analyzes the significance of the August 4th date and calls attention to the relationship of Ford's use of it and the date of England's declaration of war on Germany.

7. E. M. Forster, *Abinger Harvest* (New York, 1936), p. 5.

8. From a different perspective, Todd K. Bender comes to a similar conclusion that the way Dowell's mind reacts to the tragic events is itself a sickness. See "The Sad Tale of Dowell: Ford Madox Ford's *The Good Soldier*," *Criticism*, IV (Fall, 1962), 353-68.

Chapter Four

1. Ford Madox Ford, *The Marsden Case* (London, 1923), p. 18.
2. Ford Madox Ford, *It Was the Nightingale* (Philadelphia, 1933), p. 222.
3. Ford Madox Ford, *No More Parades* (New York, 1925), p. ix.
4. Robie Macauley, "Introduction" to *Parade's End* (New York, 1950), p. xxi.
5. Douglas Goldring, *Trained for Genius* (New York, 1949), p. 245 (italics mine).
6. See Meixner, *op. cit.*, pp. 217-21. Graham Greene in his "Introduction" to the Bodley Head edition of *Parade's End* accepts Meixner's judgment and further states that *The Last Post* was "a disaster which has delayed a full critical appreciation of *Parade's End*" (III, 5). *The Last Post* is omitted entirely from this edition on the ground that Ford himself said of it in a letter quoted in Meixner's study, "I do not like the book and have never liked it and always intended to end up with *A Man Could Stand Up—*." To take Ford literally at his word in this letter begs the question since it can be countered with Ford's contradictory statement that he intended to end *Parade's End* (referring to it as a tetralogy, not a trilogy) with *The Last Post*. The fact is he wrote the novel and published it as part of the tetralogy; it is as the concluding volume of a tetralogy that it should be judged.
7. See Meixner, *op. cit.*, p. 221. Meixner interprets the ending of *The Last Post* as a "sentimental indulgence" on Ford's part that is out of tone with the rest of the tetralogy.
8. D. H. Lawrence, *Lady Chatterley's Lover* (New York, 1959), p. 37.

Chapter Five

1. Mrs. Conrad bitterly denounced Ford's use of the material for his novel: "No one could finish it [*Suspense*] as the author intended to finish it, much less F. M. H. [Ford Madox Hueffer], who dared to declare that his book, *Little Less than Gods*, was that book completed. He knew perhaps less than most people in the literary world what my husband intended to be the finish, because, for the years from 1909, the two had been as far apart in thought as in actual personal contact" (Jessie Conrad, *Joseph Conrad and His Circle* [New York, 1935], p. 221). Mrs. Conrad, however, was antagonistic toward Ford and considered him a parasite on Conrad's reputation; therefore, her account is biased. As Wiley observes, ". . . a comparison of Conrad's book with Ford's reveals too marked a difference in emphasis and tone to justify a charge of Ford's attempting to offer a continuation of the incomplete *Suspense*" (*op. cit.*, pp. 123-24).

2. Ford Madox Ford, *When the Wicked Man* (New York, 1931), p. 179.

3. See Thomas Moser, *Conrad: Achievement—and Decline* (Cambridge, Mass., 1957).

4. See Carol Ohmann, *Ford Madox Ford: From Apprentice to Craftsman* (Middletown, Conn., 1964), pp. 175-82. Wiley alone of the major critics of Ford's novels defends the last novels as representing a development, as seen particularly in Ford's use of mythical elements and in his handling of the American scene and character.

Selected Bibliography

PRIMARY SOURCES

The Shifting of the Fire. London: T. Fisher Unwin, 1892.

Ford Madox Brown: A Record of His Life and Work. London: Longmans, Green, 1896.

The Cinque Ports: A Historical and Descriptive Record. London: Blackwood, 1900.

The Inheritors: An Extravagant Story. With Joseph Conrad. London: Heinemann, 1901.

Rossetti: A Critical Essay on His Art. London: Duckworth, 1902.

Romance. With Joseph Conrad. London: Smith, Elder, 1903; New York: McClure, Phillips, 1904.

The Benefactor: A Tale of a Small Circle. London: Brown, Langham, 1905.

Hans Holbein the Younger: A Critical Monograph. London: Duckworth, 1905.

The Fifth Queen: And How She Came to Court. London: Alston Rivers, 1906.

Privy Seal: His Last Venture. London: Alston Rivers, 1907.

England and the English: An Interpretation (Omnibus volume containing *The Soul of London*, 1905; *The Heart of the Country*, 1906; and *The Spirit of the People*, 1907). New York: McClure, Phillips, 1907.

An English Girl: A Romance. London: Methuen, 1907.

The Pre-Raphaelite Brotherhood: A Critical Monograph. London: Duckworth, 1907.

The Fifth Queen Crowned: A Romance. London: Nash, 1908.

Mr. Apollo: A Just Possible Story. London: Methuen, 1908.

The "Half Moon": A Romance of the Old World and the New. London: Nash, 1909.

A Call: The Tale of Two Passions. London: Chatto and Windus, 1910.

The Portrait. London: Methuen, 1910.

The Simple Life Limited (Published under the pseudonym of Daniel Chaucer). London: John Lane, 1911.

Ancient Lights and Certain New Reflections: Being the Memories of a Young Man. London: Chapman and Hall, 1911 (Published in America as *Memories and Impressions: A Study in Atmospheres.* New York: Harper, 1911).

Ladies Whose Bright Eyes: A Romance. London: Constable, 1911; Philadelphia: J. B. Lippincott, 1935 (revised).

The Critical Attitude. London: Duckworth, 1911.

The Panel: A Sheer Comedy. London: Constable, 1912. (Published in America as *Ring for Nancy: A Sheer Comedy.* Indianapolis: Bobbs-Merrill, 1913).

The New Humpty-Dumpty (Published under the pseudonym of Daniel Chaucer). London: John Lane, 1912.

Mr. Fleight. London: Howard Latimer, 1913.

The Young Lovell: A Romance. London: Chatto and Windus, 1913.

Henry James. London: Martin Secker, 1913; New York: Albert and Charles Boni, 1915.

The Good Soldier: A Tale of Passion. London and New York: John Lane, 1915; New York: Albert and Charles Boni, 1927; New York: Alfred A. Knopf, 1951, 1957.

Zeppelin Nights: A London Entertainment. With Violet Hunt. London: John Lane, 1915.

Thus to Revisit: Some Reminiscences. London: Chapman and Hall, 1921; New York: Dutton, 1921.

The Marsden Case: A Romance. London: Duckworth, 1923.

Some Do Not. . . . London: Duckworth, 1924; New York: Albert and Charles Boni, 1924.

The Nature of a Crime. With Joseph Conrad. London: Duckworth, 1924; New York: Doubleday, 1924, 1926.

Joseph Conrad: A Personal Remembrance. London: Duckworth, 1924; Boston: Little, Brown, 1924.

No More Parades. London: Duckworth, 1925; New York: Albert and Charles Boni, 1925.

A Man Could Stand Up—. London: Duckworth, 1926; New York: Albert and Charles Boni, 1926.

The Last Post. London: Duckworth, 1928; New York: Literary Guild of America, 1928.

A Little Less Than Gods: A Romance. London: Duckworth, 1928; New York: Viking, 1928.

The English Novel: From the Earliest Days to the Death of Conrad. Philadelphia: J. B. Lippincott, 1929; London: Constable, 1930.

Selected Bibliography

No Enemy: A Tale of Reconstruction. New York: Macaulay, 1929.

Return to Yesterday. London: Gollancz, 1931; New York: Horace Liveright, 1932.

When the Wicked Man. New York: Horace Liveright, 1931; London: Jonathan Cape, 1932.

The Rash Act. New York: Long and Smith, 1933; London: Jonathan Cape, 1933.

It Was the Nightingale. Philadelphia and London: J. B. Lippincott, 1933; London: Heinemann, 1934.

Henry for Hugh. Philadelphia and London: J. B. Lippincott, 1934.

Provence: From Minstrels to the Machine. Philadelphia and London: J. B. Lippincott, 1935; London: Allen and Unwin, 1938.

Vive Le Roy. Philadelphia and London: J. B. Lippincott, 1936.

Collected Poems. New York: Oxford University Press, 1936.

Great Trade Route. New York: Oxford University Press, 1937; London: Allen and Unwin, 1937.

Portraits from Life: Memories and Criticisms. Boston: Houghton Mifflin, 1937. (Published in England as *Mightier Than the Sword.* London: Allen and Unwin, 1938).

The March of Literature from Confucius to Modern Times. New York: Dial Press, 1938; London: Allen and Unwin, 1939.

Parade's End (The four Tietjens novels in one volume: *Some Do Not . . .* , *No More Parades, A Man Could Stand Up—, The Last Post*). New York: Alfred A. Knopf, 1950. Introduction by Robie Macauley.

The Bodley Head Ford Madox Ford. London: The Bodley Head, 1962-1963. (Four volume republication of *The Good Soldier,* selected reminiscences and poems, *The Fifth Queen* trilogy, and *Parade's End*). Edited and introduced by Graham Greene.

The Fifth Queen Trilogy. New York: Vanguard Press, 1964.

Letters of Ford Madox Ford. Edited by Richard M. Ludwig. Princeton: Princeton University Press, 1965.

SECONDARY SOURCES

Bender, Todd K. "The Sad Tale of Dowell: Ford Madox Ford's *The Good Soldier,*" *Criticism,* IV (Fall, 1962), 353-68. Suggests that the primary subject of the novel is not the story of Ashburnham but the intelligence of Dowell. The way Dowell's mind reacts to the tragic sickness around him is itself a sickness, the saddest story of all.

Bowen, Stella. *Drawn From Life*. London: Collins, 1941. Reminiscences of her life with Ford, particularly during the post-war period when he was writing *Parade's End*.

Cassell, Richard A. *Ford Madox Ford: A Study of His Novels*. Baltimore: The Johns Hopkins Press, 1961. First study to place Ford's major novels in the context of his lesser fiction. Especially good in showing the context of Ford's literary background and fictional theory.

Cox, James T. "Ford's 'Passion for Provence,'" *Journal of English Literary History*, XXVIII (December, 1961), 383-98. The single thread running throughout *The Good Soldier* is the medieval tradition of courtly love embraced by Edward Ashburnham in the twentieth century, which causes a confusion of moral values and inevitably results in tragedy.

Firebaugh, J. J. "Tietjens and the Tradition," *Pacific Spectator*, VI (Winter, 1952), 23-32. *Parade's End* as an allegory of social decay and reform.

Goldring, Douglas. *South Lodge*. London: Constable, 1943. Personal reminiscences of Ford, Violet Hunt, and the *English Review* circle.

————. *Trained for Genius*. New York: Dutton, 1949. Published as *The Last Pre-Raphaelite*. London: MacDonald, 1948. Earliest biography of Ford. Helps correct distorted view that Ford rode on the coat tails of Conrad's reputation.

Gordon, Ambrose, Jr. *The Invisible Tent: The War Novels of Ford Madox Ford*. Austin, Texas: University of Texas Press, 1964. An intensive study of Ford's war novels, with particular emphasis on *The Good Soldier* as a study of the breakdown of ordered life which anticipates the chaos of war, and on *Parade's End* as a "fairy-tale" and impressionistic rather than naturalistic treatment of war.

Gordon, Caroline. *A Good Soldier: A Key to the Novels of Ford Madox Ford*. University of California Library, Davis: Chapbook No. 1, 1963. Sees Ford's *Young Lovell* as the key to Ford's novels in its treatment of pure romance as an archetypal situation and its use of an archetypal character, the White Goddess, a Belle Dame Sans Merci.

Gose, Elliott B. "The Strange Irregular Rhythm: An Analysis of *The Good Soldier*," *Publications of the Modern Language Association*, LXXII (June, 1957), 494-509. An analysis of *The Good Soldier* with particular emphasis on evolving viewpoint of narrator as the novel progresses.

Harvey, David Dow. *Ford Madox Ford 1873-1939: A Bibliography of Works and Criticism*. Princeton: Princeton University Press, 1962. Invaluable reference tool for the student of Ford's works. Copiously annotated bibliography of works by and about Ford.

Hoffmann, Charles G. "Ford's Manuscript Revisions of *The Good Soldier*," *English Literature in Transition*, IX, 3 (1966), 145-52. A detailed discussion of the significance of Ford's manuscript revisions, including the discrepancies in dates.

Hunt, Violet. *I Have This to Say*. New York: Boni & Liveright, 1926. Published as *The Flurried Years*. London: Hurst & Blackett, 1926. Personal reminiscences about Ford and the *English Review*.

Hynes, Samuel. "The Epistemology of *The Good Soldier*," *Sewanee Review*, LXIX (Spring, 1961), 225-35. Sees Dowell's compelling need to know the truth and his developing understanding of himself and the others as the key to the novel's meaning and structure.

Lid, Richard W. *Ford Madox Ford: The Essence of His Art*. Berkeley and Los Angeles: University of California Press, 1964. Views the essence of Ford's art as his narrative method and the essence of his narrative method as style and impressionism. Places Ford in the context of his time as a truly transitional writer from the 19th to the 20th century.

Ludwig, Richard M. "The Reputation of Ford Madox Ford," *Publications of the Modern Language Association*, LXXVI (December, 1961), 544-51. Traces Ford's disregard for facts to his impressionism, and his unfavorable reputation as a biographer to the reader's failure to understand his intentions to convey impressions not facts.

Macauley, Robie. "The Good Ford," *Kenyon Review*, XI (Spring, 1949), 269-88. Separates the "good" Ford novels from the "bad," with particular emphasis on an analysis of *The Good Soldier* and *Parade's End*.

————. "Introduction" to *Parade's End*. New York: Knopf, 1950, pp. v-xxii. *Parade's End* viewed "as one novel divided into four different books."

MacShane, Frank. "Ford Madox Ford and His Contemporaries: Techniques of the Novel," *English Studies in Transition*, IV, 1 (1961), 2-11. Emphasizes Ford's interest in the techniques of the novel as opposed to moral purpose, comparing his theories with those of Conrad, James, Galsworthy, Bennett, and Wells.

————. "A Conscious Craftsman: Ford Madox Ford's Manuscript Revisions," *Boston University Studies in English*, V (Autumn, 1961), 178-84. Of particular interest in showing Ford's manuscript revisions of *Some Do Not.* . . .

————. *The Life and Works of Ford Madox Ford*. New York: Horizon Press, 1965. A well-written and well-documented account of Ford's life which supplements Goldring's earlier biography, but critical commentary on the novels is disappointing when compared with the several critical studies recently published.

Meixner, John A. *Ford Madox Ford's Novels: A Critical Study*. Minneapolis: University of Minnesota Press, 1961. Considers *The Good Soldier* Ford's masterpiece, but considers *Parade's End* a failure as a multiple novel although *Some Do Not* . . . is viewed as a separate, single masterpiece.

Modern Fiction Studies, IX (Spring, 1963). Whole issue devoted to Ford. Among the articles the following are particularly recommended: Marlene Griffith, "A Double Reading of *Parade's End*"; Patricia McFate and Bruce Golden, "*The Good Soldier*: A Tragedy of Self Deception"; Ambrose Gordon, Jr., "At the Edge of Silence: *The Good Soldier* as 'War Novel.'" Contains selected checklist of criticism of Ford.

New Directions: Number 7. Norfolk, Conn.: New Directions, 1942. Reminiscences and appraisals by many who knew Ford, including Richard Aldington, Ezra Pound, Caroline Gordon, John Peale Bishop, William Carlos Williams, Granville Hicks.

Ohmann, Carol. *Ford Madox Ford: From Apprentice to Craftsman*. Middletown, Conn.: Wesleyan University Press, 1964. Although none of Ford's early novels is recommended, all are seen as an apprenticeship leading to the achievement of *The Good Soldier* and *Parade's End*. Late novels regarded as an unhappy epilogue.

Schorer, Mark. "An Interpretation," *The Good Soldier*. New York: Knopf, 1951, pp. v-xv. Published originally in *The Princeton University Library Chronicle*, IX (April, 1948), 128-33. Interprets Ford's "saddest story" as a work of comic irony.

Wiley, Paul L. *Novelist of Three Worlds: Ford Madox Ford*. Syracuse, N. Y.: Syracuse University Press, 1962. Seeks to show a pattern of continuous development in Ford's career from early to late novels. Analyzes "the elements of the Affair" leading to the "perfected Affair" of *The Good Soldier*.

Index

Index